Low Cholesterol Diet Cookbook for Beginners

2000 Days of Quick, Easy, and Delicious Recipes with Pictures to Boost Heart Health, Reduce Cholesterol Naturally, and a 4-Week Meal Plan

dr. YOLANDA GILL

CONTENTS

WELCOME!

Thank you for purchasing the Low Cholesterol Cookbook for Beginners. This cookbook has been crafted to help you enjoy delicious and heart-healthy meals while maintaining a low cholesterol diet.

Getting Started: Familiarize Yourself with Heart-Healthy Cooking Techniques: Before starting with the recipes, take some time to understand key heart-healthy cooking methods such as steaming, grilling, baking, and sautéing with minimal oil. These techniques are essential for maintaining flavor while keeping cholesterol levels in check.

Read Through Each Recipe: Each recipe includes a list of ingredients, step-by-step cooking instructions, and nutritional information. Carefully review these sections to make sure you have all the necessary ingredients and understand the cooking process.

Use the Conversion Table: The cookbook includes a conversion table to help you accurately measure ingredients. This can be especially useful if you want to adjust the recipe to make more or fewer servings than originally provided.

Adapting Recipes: If you need to adjust the number of servings, use the conversion table to ensure that all ingredient quantities are modified accordingly. Please note that cooking times may vary when making significant changes to the ingredient amounts.

Incorporating Your Favorite Ingredients: Feel free to add herbs, spices, or vegetables that you love, or substitute ingredients to suit your taste. This can help you personalize your meals while keeping them heart-healthy.

Adjusting Cooking Times: Keep in mind that cooking times may vary depending on your cooking equipment and the amount of food being prepared. It's always a good idea to start with the suggested cooking time and adjust as needed, checking for doneness.

Note on Recipe Photos: Some of the photos in this cookbook have been styled to enhance visual appeal. Additional ingredients or different cutting techniques may have been used to create a more attractive presentation. These variations are intended for aesthetic purposes only and do not alter the nutritional profile or core ingredients of the recipes.

As you embark on this journey toward a healthier lifestyle, remember that the goal of these recipes is to make healthy eating enjoyable and accessible. The low-cholesterol dishes in this cookbook are designed to be both flavorful and beneficial for your heart health. Experiment with flavors, have fun in the kitchen, and savor every bite.

Enjoy your cooking and stay heart-healthy!

Welcome to the **Low Cholesterol Cookbook for Beginners**, your comprehensive guide to embracing a heart-healthy lifestyle without sacrificing flavor or enjoyment. As a nutritionist, I understand that managing cholesterol levels can feel daunting, but with the right knowledge and tools, it becomes an empowering journey toward better health. This cookbook is designed to help you navigate the world of low-cholesterol eating by providing delicious recipes, practical advice, and evidence-based information to support your wellness goals.

High cholesterol is a significant risk factor for cardiovascular diseases, which remain a leading cause of mortality worldwide. The good news is that diet plays a crucial role in managing cholesterol levels. By making informed food choices and adopting healthy cooking techniques, you can lower your cholesterol naturally while enjoying satisfying meals. This book aims to debunk the myth that healthy eating is bland or restrictive, showcasing a variety of flavorful dishes that are as delightful to your taste buds as they are beneficial to your heart.

Understanding Cholesterol

What Is Cholesterol, and How Does Diet Impact It?

Cholesterol is a waxy, fat-like substance found in every cell of your body. It's essential for producing hormones, vitamin D, and substances that aid digestion. Your liver produces all the cholesterol your body needs, but cholesterol is also introduced through dietary sources, particularly animal-based foods.

There are two primary types of cholesterol carried through your bloodstream by lipoproteins:

- **Low-Density Lipoprotein (LDL):** Often referred to as "bad" cholesterol, LDL carries cholesterol particles throughout your body. High levels of LDL can lead to cholesterol buildup in your arteries, forming plaques that increase the risk of heart disease and stroke.

- **High-Density Lipoprotein (HDL):** Known as "good" cholesterol, HDL helps transport excess cholesterol back to your liver, where it's processed and removed from your body. Higher levels of HDL are associated with a lower risk of heart disease.

Diet impacts cholesterol levels significantly. Consuming foods high in saturated fats, trans fats, and dietary cholesterol can raise your LDL levels. Conversely, eating foods rich in unsaturated fats, fiber, and plant sterols can help lower LDL levels and raise HDL levels. Understanding how different foods affect your cholesterol is the first step toward making heart-healthy choices.

How to Use Diet to Reduce Cholesterol Naturally

Reducing cholesterol naturally involves incorporating certain foods and nutrients while limiting others:

- **Increase Soluble Fiber Intake:** Foods like oats, barley, legumes, apples, and berries contain soluble fiber, which binds to cholesterol in your digestive system and helps remove it from your body.

- **Choose Healthy Fats:** Replace saturated and trans fats with monounsaturated and polyunsaturated fats found in olive oil, avocados, nuts, seeds, and fatty fish like salmon and mackerel.

- **Incorporate Plant Sterols and Stanols:** Naturally occurring in fruits, vegetables, nuts, and whole grains, these substances help block the absorption of cholesterol.

- **Limit Dietary Cholesterol:** Reduce consumption of high-cholesterol foods such as red meat, full-fat dairy products, and processed meats.

- **Opt for Lean Proteins:** Choose skinless poultry, fish, legumes, and tofu over fatty cuts of meat.

- **Reduce Sugar and Refined Carbohydrates:** High intake of sugar and refined carbs can lower HDL (good cholesterol) and raise triglycerides, contributing to heart disease.

- **Maintain a Healthy Weight:** Weight loss can help lower LDL cholesterol and triglycerides while raising HDL cholesterol.

The Principles of a Low-Cholesterol Diet

Explanation of the Key Food Groups

A low-cholesterol diet emphasizes nutrient-dense foods that support cardiovascular health:

Healthy Fats
- **Monounsaturated Fats:** Found in olive oil, canola oil, avocados, and most nuts. These fats help reduce LDL cholesterol levels and maintain HDL cholesterol.
- **Polyunsaturated Fats:** Including omega-3 and omega-6 fatty acids found in fatty fish, flaxseeds, walnuts, and sunflower seeds. Omega-3 fatty acids, in particular, have anti-inflammatory properties and support heart health.

Lean Proteins
- **Fish:** Rich in omega-3 fatty acids, especially salmon, trout, and sardines.
- **Poultry:** Skinless chicken or turkey provides protein with less saturated fat.
- **Plant-Based Proteins:** Beans, lentils, chickpeas, tofu, and tempeh are excellent sources of protein and fiber without cholesterol.

Complex Carbohydrates
- **Whole Grains:** Oats, brown rice, quinoa, barley, and whole wheat bread are high in fiber, which helps lower LDL cholesterol.
- **Vegetables and Fruits:** Provide essential vitamins, minerals, antioxidants, and fiber. Aim for a variety of colors to ensure a wide range of nutrients.

Nuts and Seeds
- Almonds, walnuts, flaxseeds, and chia seeds contribute healthy fats, protein, and fiber.

Low-Fat Dairy or Dairy Alternatives
- Choose low-fat or non-fat milk, yogurt, and cheese, or opt for plant-based alternatives like almond or soy milk fortified with calcium and vitamin D.

How to Balance Meals for Both Nutrition and Taste

Creating balanced meals that are both nutritious and flavorful involves:

Combining Food Groups: Each meal should include a balance of proteins, healthy fats, and complex carbohydrates.

- **Portion Control:** Be mindful of serving sizes to avoid overeating, which can contribute to weight gain and negatively impact cholesterol levels.

- **Colorful Plates**: Incorporate a variety of fruits and vegetables to make meals visually appealing and nutrient-rich.

- **Flavor Enhancements:** Use herbs, spices, and natural seasonings to enhance taste without adding unhealthy fats or excess sodium.

The Role of Portion Control and Mindful Eating

- **Portion Control:**
  - Understanding Serving Sizes: Familiarize yourself with recommended serving sizes for different food groups.
  - Using Smaller Plates: This visual trick can help you feel satisfied with smaller portions.
  - Avoiding Second Helpings: Allow time for your body to register fullness before considering additional servings.

- **Mindful Eating:**
  - Eating Slowly: Take time to chew thoroughly and savor each bite, which can improve digestion and satiety.
  - Eliminating Distractions: Focus on your meal without the interference of televisions or smartphones.
  - Listening to Hunger Cues: Eat when you're hungry and stop when you're comfortably full.

The Importance of Flavor in a Low-Cholesterol Diet

Tips for Using Herbs, Spices, and Other Natural Flavor Enhancers
Flavorful food doesn't have to rely on unhealthy fats or excessive salt. Enhancing the taste of your meals naturally can make healthy eating enjoyable:

- **Herbs and Spices:**
  - **Fresh Herbs:** Basil, cilantro, parsley, rosemary, thyme, and dill add brightness and depth.
  - **Spices:** Turmeric, cumin, paprika, cinnamon, and ginger provide warmth and complexity.

- **Aromatics:**
  - **Onions and Garlic:** Fundamental for building flavor bases in many cuisines.
  - **Peppers:** Bell peppers, chili peppers, and jalapeños can add sweetness or heat.

- **Citrus and Vinegars:**
  - **Lemon and Lime Juice:** Brighten flavors and can reduce the need for added salt.
  - **Balsamic, Apple Cider, and Rice Vinegar:** Add acidity and depth to dressings and marinades.

- **Umami-Rich Ingredients:**
  - **Mushrooms, Tomatoes, and Soy Sauce:** Provide savory notes that enhance satisfaction.

How to Use Herbs, Spices, and Seasonings

How to Use Spices to Create Bold, Flavorful Dishes Without Relying on Fat or Cholesterol
- **Building Flavor Layers:**
  - Start with Aromatics: Sauté onions, garlic, and ginger to create a flavor foundation.
  - Bloom Spices: Cook dried spices briefly in oil to release their essential oils.

- **Creating Homemade Spice Blends:**
  - Mediterranean Blend:
    - Ingredients: Oregano, basil, thyme, rosemary, garlic powder, lemon zest.
    - Uses: Season chicken, fish, vegetables, and salads.
  - Mexican Blend:
    - Ingredients: Cumin, chili powder, smoked paprika, coriander, oregano.
    - Uses: Flavor beans, rice, grilled meats, and salsas.
  - Asian-Inspired Blend:
    - Ingredients: Five-spice powder, ground ginger, garlic powder, white pepper.
    - Uses: Stir-fries, marinades, and soups.

- **Balancing Flavors:**
  - Sweetness: Use a touch of honey or maple syrup to balance acidity or heat.
  - Acidity: Add vinegar or citrus juice to brighten flavors.

Examples of Spice Blends to Add Variety to Meals
- **Curry Powder:**
  - A blend of turmeric, cumin, coriander, fenugreek, and chili peppers.
  - Uses: Flavor lentil dishes, soups, and roasted vegetables.
- **Italian Seasoning:**
  - A mix of basil, oregano, rosemary, thyme, and marjoram.
  - Uses: Enhance pasta sauces, grilled vegetables, and poultry.
- **Cajun Spice Mix:**
  - Combines paprika, cayenne pepper, garlic powder, onion powder, black pepper, and oregano.
  - Uses: Season seafood, chicken, and rice dishes.

Healthy Fat Substitutes

How to Use Healthy Fats Like Olive Oil, Avocado, and Nuts in Moderation to Enhance Flavor
- **Olive Oil:**
  - Usage: Drizzle over salads, use in marinades, or for light sautéing.
  - Portion Control: Use a measuring spoon to control the amount; 1-2 teaspoons per serving is sufficient.
- **Avocado:**
  - Usage: Mash as a spread, slice into salads, or blend into dressings.
  - Benefits: Provides creaminess and richness without cholesterol.
- **Nuts and Seeds:**
  - Usage: Sprinkle chopped nuts over oatmeal, yogurt, or salads.
  - Portion Control: Stick to a small handful (about 1 ounce) to manage calorie intake.

Tips for Reducing or Replacing Butter, Cream, and Cheese Without Sacrificing Taste
- **Butter Alternatives:**

- Mashed Fruit: Use unsweetened applesauce or mashed bananas in baking.
- Plant-Based Spreads: Choose those without hydrogenated oils.
- **Cream Substitutes:**
  - Greek Yogurt: Use non-fat or low-fat varieties in sauces and dressings.
  - Silken Tofu: Blend into soups and smoothies for creaminess.
- **Cheese Replacements:**
  - Nutritional Yeast: Provides a cheesy flavor in sauces and toppings.
  - Herbed Purees: Blend cashews or white beans with herbs as a spread or dip.
- **Enhancing Flavor and Texture:**
  - Spices and Herbs: Compensate for reduced fats with flavorful seasonings.
  - Roasting and Grilling: Develop natural flavors in ingredients.

Conclusion

Transitioning to a low-cholesterol diet is a meaningful step toward improving your heart health and overall well-being. By embracing whole, nutrient-rich foods and employing flavorful cooking techniques, you can enjoy satisfying meals that support your health goals. Remember that small, consistent changes can lead to significant long-term benefits.

This guide provides you with the foundational knowledge to confidently begin your journey. By planning your meals, stocking your pantry wisely, and experimenting with herbs and spices, you'll find that a low-cholesterol diet is not only manageable but also enjoyable.

Empower yourself with these tools and embrace the flavorful, heart-healthy possibilities that await you. Your journey to better health starts with the choices you make today, and this cookbook is here to support you every step of the way.

1 GALLON:
4 Quarts
8 Pints
16 Cups
128 Ounces
3.8 Liters

1 QUART:
2 Pints
4 Cups
32 Ounces
.95 Liters

1 PINT:
2 Cups
16 Ounces
480 mL

MEASURE .... EQUIVALENT

t = teaspoon • Tbsp = tablespoon

1/16 tsp	dash
1/8 tsp	a pinch
3 tsps	1 Tbsp
1/8 cup	2 Tbsps (= 1 standard coffee scoop)
1/4 cup	4 Tbsps
1/3 cup	5 Tbsps + 1 tsp
1/2 cup	8 Tbsps
3/4 cup	12 Tbsps
1 cup	16 Tbsps

1 Bushel = 4 Pecks

1 CUP:
16 Tbsp
1/2 Pint
8 Ounces
240 mL

1/4 CUP:
4 Tbsp
12 tsp
2 Ounces
60 mL

1 Tbsp:
3 tsp
1/2 Ounce
15 mL

1 STICK BUTTER:
Volume............1/2 cup /125 mL
Weight ....1/4 lb (4 oz)/115 g

SUBSTITUTIONS

HERBS:
1Tbsp fresh = 1 tsp dry

1 EGG:
1Tbsp ground flax OR chia seed + 3 Tbsp water
4 Tbsp applesauce
1/2 of a medium mashed banana

1 CUP BUTTERMILK:
1 tbsp lemon juice or vinegar + enough milk to equal 1 cup (for baking, let stand for a few minutes before using)

1 CUP OF SUGAR:
3/4 cup honey
3/4 cup maple syrup
2/3 cup agave nectar
1 tsp. stevia

- For honey, decrease liquid by 2-4 tsp., add a pinch of baking soda and decrease oven temp by 25 degrees
- For maple syrup, decrease liquid by 3 tbsp., add 1/4 tsp. of baking soda per cup of syrup and decrease oven temp by 25 degrees
- For agave nectar, decrease liquid by 1/4 cup, increase cook time by 6% and decrease oven temp by 25 degrees
- For stevia, to replace missing bulk, use applesauce, apple butter or yogurt

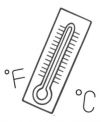

OVEN TEMPERATURE

FARENHEIT	CELSIUS
275º F	140º C
300º F	150º C
325º F	165º C
350º F	180º C
375º F	190º C
400º F	200º C
425º F	220º C
450º F	230º C
475º F	240º C

BREAKFEST

Berry Burst Oatmeal with Almond Crunch

 5 min 10 min 2 svgs.

Ingredients:

- 1 cup rolled oats (preferably whole grain)
- 2 cups unsweetened almond milk (or any plant-based milk)
- 1 tablespoon ground flaxseeds (optional for extra fiber)
- 1 teaspoon vanilla extract
- 1/2 teaspoon ground cinnamon (plus extra for garnish)
- 1/2 cup fresh mixed berries (blueberries, raspberries, strawberries)
- 2 tablespoons sliced almonds (lightly toasted)
- 1 tablespoon honey or maple syrup (optional for sweetness)
- Fresh mint leaves (optional for garnish)

Instructions:

1. Prepare the Oatmeal Base:
In a medium saucepan, combine the rolled oats and almond milk. Bring to a gentle boil over medium heat, stirring occasionally. Once the mixture starts to boil, reduce the heat to low and simmer for 5-7 minutes, stirring frequently until the oats are soft and creamy.

2. Add Flavor:
Stir in the vanilla extract, ground cinnamon, and ground flaxseeds (if using). Continue cooking for another minute until the flavors are well combined.

3. Prepare the Almond Crunch:
While the oats are simmering, toast the sliced almonds in a small dry skillet over medium heat. Stir frequently for 2-3 minutes until they are golden brown and fragrant. Remove from heat and set aside.

4. Assemble the Oatmeal:
Once the oatmeal reaches your desired consistency, remove it from the heat. Divide the oatmeal evenly between two bowls. Top each bowl with a generous serving of fresh mixed berries, toasted almonds, and an optional drizzle of honey or maple syrup.

5. Garnish and Serve:
Garnish the oatmeal with a sprinkle of additional cinnamon and fresh mint leaves for a touch of brightness. Serve warm.

Nutr. (Per Serving): Calories: 320 | Prot: 8g | Carbs: 45g | Fat: 12g | Fiber: 9g | Chol: 0mg | Na: 170mg | K: 290mg

Spinach and Mushroom Egg White Omelette

 5 min 10 min 2 svgs.

Ingredients:

- 3 large egg whites
- 1/2 cup fresh spinach leaves (roughly chopped)
- 1/4 cup sliced mushrooms (white or cremini)
- 1 tablespoon olive oil (or cooking spray for a lower-fat option)
- 1/4 teaspoon garlic powder
- Salt and pepper to taste
- Fresh parsley for garnish (optional)
- 1 slice whole wheat toast (optional, for serving)
- 1/4 avocado, sliced (optional, for serving)

Instructions:

1. Prepare the Filling:
Heat the olive oil in a non-stick skillet over medium heat. Add the sliced mushrooms and sauté for 3-4 minutes until softened. Add the chopped spinach to the skillet and sauté for another 1-2 minutes until wilted. Season with garlic powder, salt, and pepper. Remove the vegetables from the pan and set aside.

2. Cook the Egg Whites:
In the same skillet, pour the egg whites evenly across the pan. Cook over medium heat for 2-3 minutes or until the eggs begin to set around the edges. Gently lift the edges of the egg whites with a spatula and allow any uncooked egg whites to flow underneath.

3. Assemble the Omelette:
Once the egg whites are mostly set, spoon the sautéed spinach and mushroom mixture onto one half of the omelette. Carefully fold the other half of the omelette over the filling. Cook for an additional minute to ensure the egg whites are fully cooked and the filling is warm.

4. Serve:
Slide the omelette onto a plate and garnish with fresh parsley, if desired. Serve with a slice of whole wheat toast and sliced avocado on the side for added heart-healthy fats and fiber.

Nutr. (Per Serving): Calories: 220 | Prot: 15g | Carbs: 12g | Fat: 12g | Fiber: 5g | Chol: 0mg | Na: 250mg | K: 480mg

Greek Yogurt Parfait with Honey and Berries

Ingredients:

- 1 cup plain, non-fat Greek yogurt
- 1/2 cup fresh mixed berries (blueberries, raspberries, strawberries)
- 1 tablespoon honey (or maple syrup for a vegan option)
- 2 tablespoons granola (low-fat, low-sugar)
- 1 teaspoon chia seeds or flaxseeds (optional for extra fiber)
- Fresh mint leaves for garnish (optional)

Customizable Options:

- Berries: Swap out berries for other fruits like peaches, kiwi, or mango.
- Granola: Use crushed nuts or seeds if you prefer a grain-free option.
- Sweetener: Replace honey with agave syrup or keep it unsweetened.

Instructions:

1. Prepare the Base:
In a clear glass or bowl, spoon half of the Greek yogurt into the bottom, spreading it evenly.
2. Layer with Berries and Honey:
Add a layer of mixed fresh berries over the yogurt, followed by a drizzle of honey.
3. Repeat the Layers:
Add the remaining Greek yogurt on top of the berry layer, followed by more berries and another drizzle of honey.
4. Top with Crunch:
Sprinkle the granola over the top, and if desired, add chia seeds or flaxseeds for an extra nutritional boost.

5. Garnish and Serve:
Garnish the parfait with a few fresh mint leaves for a burst of freshness. Serve immediately and enjoy!

Nutr. (Per Serving): Calories: 250 | Prot: 18g | Carbs: 35g | Fat: 5g | Fiber: 6g | Chol: 0mg | Na: 100mg | K: 400mg

Veggie-Packed Breakfast Burrito Wrap

Ingredients:

- 4 large egg whites
- 1/2 cup bell peppers (sliced)
- 1/2 cup onions (sliced)
- 1 cup fresh spinach leaves
- 1 tablespoon olive oil (or cooking spray for less fat)
- 2 whole wheat tortillas (8-inch)
- 1/2 avocado (sliced)
- 2 tablespoons salsa (optional)
- Fresh cilantro for garnish (optional)
- Salt and pepper to taste

Customizable Options:

- Protein Additions: Add black beans or tofu for extra protein.
- Spices: Add cumin, smoked paprika, or chili flakes for a kick.
- Toppings: Top with Greek yogurt or low-fat cheese for a creamier texture.

Instructions:

1. Sauté the Vegetables:
Heat the olive oil in a non-stick skillet over medium heat. Add the bell peppers and onions, and sauté for 3-4 minutes until softened. Add the spinach and cook for another 1-2 minutes until wilted. Season with salt and pepper to taste. Remove from the skillet and set aside.
2. Cook the Egg Whites:
In the same skillet, add the egg whites and cook over medium heat, stirring gently until scrambled and fully set. This should take about 2-3 minutes.
3. Assemble the Burritos:
Warm the whole wheat tortillas in a dry skillet or microwave for

about 10 seconds to make them pliable. Place half of the scrambled egg whites and sautéed vegetables in the center of each tortilla. Add a few slices of avocado on top and drizzle with salsa if desired.
4. Wrap and Serve:
Fold in the sides of the tortilla, then roll it up from one end to the other to create a burrito. Slice in half if preferred. Garnish with fresh cilantro and serve immediately.

Nutr. (Per Serving): Calories: 300 | Prot: 15g | Carbs: 30g | Fat: 12g | Fiber: 7g | Chol: 0mg | Na: 280mg | K: 600mg

Sweet Potato and Black Bean Breakfast Hash

Ingredients:

- 1 medium sweet potato, peeled and diced (about 2 cups)
- 1 tablespoon olive oil (or cooking spray for a lower-fat option)
- 1/2 cup black beans (cooked or canned, drained and rinsed)
- 1/2 red bell pepper, diced
- 1/4 cup red onion, finely chopped
- 1/2 teaspoon ground cumin
- 1/2 teaspoon smoked paprika
- Salt and pepper to taste
- Fresh cilantro for garnish (optional)
- Lime wedges for serving (optional)

Customizable Options:
- Add protein: Top with scrambled egg whites or tofu for extra protein.
- Spices: Add chili powder or cayenne pepper for a spicy kick.
- Toppings: Serve with avocado slices or a dollop of low-fat Greek yogurt.

Instructions:

1. Roast the Sweet Potatoes:

Preheat the oven to 400°F (200°C). Toss the diced sweet potatoes with 1/2 tablespoon of olive oil, cumin, smoked paprika, salt, and pepper. Spread them evenly on a baking sheet. Roast for 15-20 minutes, flipping halfway through, until the sweet potatoes are tender and golden brown.

2. Sauté the Vegetables and Beans:

While the sweet potatoes are roasting, heat the remaining olive oil in a non-stick skillet over medium heat. Add the red bell pepper and red onion, sautéing for 3-4 minutes until softened. Stir in the black beans and cook for another 2-3 minutes until heated through. Season with a pinch of salt and pepper.

3. Combine and Serve:

Once the sweet potatoes are done, add them to the skillet with the black beans and vegetables. Toss everything together and cook for another minute to combine the flavors.

Transfer the hash to plates and garnish with fresh cilantro. Serve with lime wedges for a zesty finish.

Nutr. (Per Serving): Calories: 250 | Prot: 6g | Carbs: 40g | Fat: 7g | Fiber: 10g | Chol: 0mg | Na: 230mg | K: 750mg

Fluffy Whole Wheat Pancakes with Fresh Strawberries

Ingredients:

- 1 cup whole wheat flour
- 1 tablespoon baking powder
- 1 tablespoon ground flaxseed (optional for extra fiber)
- 1 tablespoon honey or maple syrup
- 1/2 teaspoon vanilla extract
- 1/4 teaspoon salt
- 1 cup unsweetened almond milk (or any plant-based milk)
- 1 tablespoon olive oil (or cooking spray for less fat)
- 1/2 cup fresh strawberries, sliced
- 1/4 cup plain non-fat Greek yogurt (optional for serving)
- 1 tablespoon honey or maple syrup (optional for topping)
- Fresh mint leaves for garnish (optional)

Instructions:

1. Prepare the Batter:

In a large bowl, whisk together the whole wheat flour, baking powder, ground flaxseed (if using), and salt. In a separate bowl, mix the almond milk, olive oil, honey, and vanilla extract until well combined. Pour the wet ingredients into the dry ingredients and stir until just combined. Be careful not to overmix the batter—small lumps are fine.

2. Cook the Pancakes:

Heat a non-stick skillet or griddle over medium heat. Lightly grease the skillet with a small amount of olive oil or cooking spray. Pour about 1/4 cup of batter onto the skillet for each pancake. Cook for 2-3 minutes or until bubbles form on the surface, then flip and cook for another 2 minutes until golden brown and cooked through.

3. Serve:

Stack the pancakes on a plate, and top with fresh strawberries. Optionally, drizzle with honey or maple syrup, and serve with a dollop of plain non-fat Greek yogurt on the side.

Garnish with fresh mint leaves for a colorful and refreshing touch.

Nutr. (Per Serving): Calories: 220 | Prot: 6g | Carbs: 38g | Fat: 6g | Fiber: 6g | Chol: 0mg | Na: 230mg | K: 210mg

Tofu Scramble with Peppers and Onions

⏱ 10 min | 🍳 10 min | 🍽 2 svgs.

Ingredients:

- 1 block (14 oz) firm tofu, drained and crumbled
- 1 tablespoon olive oil (or cooking spray for less fat)
- 1/2 red bell pepper, diced
- 1/2 yellow bell pepper, diced
- 1/4 cup red onion, diced
- 1/2 teaspoon turmeric (for color and flavor)
- 1/2 teaspoon cumin powder
- 1/4 teaspoon smoked paprika

- Salt and pepper to taste
- Fresh parsley or cilantro for garnish
- Optional: 1/2 avocado (for serving)
- Optional: Whole grain toast (for serving)

Instructions:

1. **Prepare the Tofu:**
Drain the tofu and pat it dry with a paper towel. Crumble the tofu into small, bite-sized pieces with your hands or a fork. Set aside.
2. **Sauté the Vegetables:**
Heat the olive oil in a non-stick skillet over medium heat. Add the diced bell peppers and onions, and sauté for 3-4 minutes until softened and lightly browned.
3. **Add the Tofu:**
Push the vegetables to the side of the skillet and add the crumbled tofu. Stir in the turmeric, cumin, smoked paprika, salt, and pepper. Cook for 5-7 minutes, stirring occasionally, until the tofu is golden and heated through. Mix the tofu and vegetables together to combine the flavors.
4. **Serve:**
   - Once cooked, remove the skillet from the heat. Garnish with fresh parsley or cilantro. Serve with sliced avocado and whole grain toast on the side for a complete, heart-healthy meal.

Nutr. (Per Serving): Calories: 220 | Prot: 14g | Carbs: 12g | Fat: 12g | Fiber: 6g | Chol: 0mg | Na: 220mg | K: 450mg

Smoked Salmon and Avocado English Muffin

⏱ 2 min | 🍳 0 min | 🍽 1 svgs.

Ingredients:

- 1 whole grain English muffin, split and toasted
- 1/2 ripe avocado, mashed
- 2 oz smoked salmon
- Fresh dill, for garnish
- Black pepper, to taste
- Lemon wedge (optional, for drizzling)
- Optional: A small handful of baby spinach or arugula for extra greens

Customizable Options:
- Add capers: For a salty, tangy flavor.
- Substitute smoked salmon: Try smoked trout or a plant-based option if preferred.
- Top with: Sliced cucumber or radish for added crunch.

Instructions:

1. **Toast the Muffin:**
Split the whole grain English muffin in half and lightly toast it until golden brown.
2. **Prepare the Avocado:**
Mash the avocado in a small bowl. Season with a pinch of black pepper and spread it evenly over both halves of the toasted muffin.
3. **Add the Smoked Salmon:**
Layer the smoked salmon slices on top of the mashed avocado.
4. **Garnish and Serve:**
Garnish with fresh dill and an extra sprinkle of black pepper.

Squeeze a little lemon juice over the top, if desired. For an extra touch, serve with a small side of greens like baby spinach or arugula.

Nutr. (Per Serving): Calories: 310 | Prot: 17g | Carbs: 30g | Fat: 15g | Fiber: 8g | Chol: 30mg | Na: 670mg | K: 600mg

Egg White Frittata with Asparagus and Herbs

10 min | 20 min | 4 svgs.

Ingredients:

- 8 large egg whites
- 1 tablespoon olive oil (or cooking spray for less fat)
- 1 cup asparagus, trimmed and cut into 1-inch pieces
- 1/4 cup onion, finely chopped
- 1/4 cup fresh herbs (parsley, chives, or dill)
- 1/2 teaspoon garlic powder
- Salt and pepper to taste

- Optional: 1/4 cup low-fat feta cheese or grated parmesan for added flavor

Customizable Options:
- Vegetables: Add bell peppers, spinach, or cherry tomatoes for extra color and nutrition.
- Herbs: Customize with fresh basil, thyme, or tarragon for a different flavor profile.
- Toppings: Serve with a side of mixed greens or a light vinaigrette.

Instructions:

1. Prepare the Vegetables:
Preheat the oven to 350°F (180°C). Heat olive oil in a non-stick, oven-safe skillet over medium heat. Add the asparagus and onions, and sauté for 3-4 minutes until the asparagus is tender and the onions are soft.

2. Mix the Egg Whites:
In a medium bowl, whisk the egg whites with garlic powder, salt, and pepper. Stir in half of the fresh herbs.

3. Cook the Frittata:
Pour the egg white mixture over the sautéed vegetables in the skillet. Cook on the stove over medium heat for 2-3 minutes until the edges start to set. Transfer the skillet to the preheated oven

and bake for 10-12 minutes until the frittata is set in the middle and lightly golden.

4. Serve:
Remove the frittata from the oven and let it cool for a minute. Garnish with the remaining fresh herbs and, if desired, sprinkle with a little low-fat cheese. Slice into wedges and serve with a side of fresh greens or whole-grain toast for a complete meal.

Nutr. (Per Serving): Calories: 120 | Prot: 12g | Carbs: 4g | Fat: 5g | Fiber: 1g | Chol: 0mg | Na: 210mg | K: 300mg

Whole Grain Bagel with Tofu Cream Cheese and Chives

5 min | 3 min | 1 svgs.

Ingredients:

- 1 whole grain bagel (split and toasted)
- 1/4 cup tofu cream cheese (store-bought or homemade)
- 1 tbsp fresh chives, finely chopped
- 1 tsp lemon juice (optional for added tang)
- Pinch of black pepper to taste
- Fresh herbs (e.g., dill or parsley, for garnish)

Customizable Options:
- Avocado slices: Add for extra healthy fats and creaminess.
- Tomato slices: For added texture and flavor.
- Cucumber slices: Adds a refreshing crunch.
- Red pepper flakes: For a slight kick of heat.

Instructions:

1. Toast the Bagel:
Split the whole grain bagel in half and lightly toast it until golden brown. Toasting enhances the nutty flavor and adds a satisfying crunch.

2. Prepare the Tofu Cream Cheese Spread:
In a small bowl, combine the tofu cream cheese with finely chopped chives and lemon juice, if using. Stir until smooth and creamy. Season with a pinch of black pepper.

3. Assemble the Bagel:
Spread a generous layer of the tofu cream cheese mixture onto both halves of the toasted bagel.

4. Garnish and Serve:
Garnish with fresh herbs like dill or parsley for added flavor and visual appeal. Serve with avocado slices or cherry tomatoes on the side, if desired.

Nutr. (Per Serving): Calories: 270 | Prot: 12g | Carbs: 40g | Fat: 8g | Fiber: 7g | Chol: 0mg | Na: 290mg | K: 180mg

Tomato Basil Egg Muffins

⏱ 10 min 🍳 15 min 🍽 3 svgs.

Ingredients:

- 6 large egg whites
- 1/2 cup cherry tomatoes, diced
- 1/4 cup fresh basil, chopped
- 1/4 cup low-fat mozzarella cheese, shredded (optional)
- 1/4 tsp garlic powder
- Salt and pepper to taste
- Non-stick cooking spray

- Customizable Options:
- Add spinach or bell peppers for extra veggies.
- Substitute low-fat cheese with nutritional yeast for a dairy-free option.
- Add chili flakes for a little heat.

Instructions:

1. Preheat the Oven:
 Preheat your oven to 350°F (175°C) and lightly grease a muffin tin with non-stick cooking spray.
2. Prepare the Egg Mixture:
 In a medium bowl, whisk the egg whites until slightly frothy. Stir in the garlic powder, salt, and pepper to season.
3. Assemble the Muffins:
 Evenly distribute the diced tomatoes and chopped basil among the muffin tin cups. If you're using cheese, sprinkle a small amount into each cup as well.
4. Pour the Egg Whites:
 Carefully pour the egg whites into the muffin tin, filling each cup about 3/4 full to allow room for the muffins to rise.
5. Bake:
 Place the muffin tin in the preheated oven and bake for 12-15 minutes or until the egg muffins are fully set and slightly golden on top.
6. Cool and Serve:
 Allow the muffins to cool slightly before removing them from the tin. Garnish with fresh basil leaves for an extra touch of flavor. Enjoy warm or at room temperature.

Nutr. (Per Serving): Calories: 70 | Prot: 9g | Carbs: 2g | Fat: 2g | Fiber: 0.5g | Chol: 0mg | Na: 120mg | K: 190mg

Almond Butter and Banana Whole Grain Wrap

⏱ 5 min 🍳 0 min 🍽 1 svgs.

Ingredients:

- 1 whole grain tortilla (preferably 8-inch, low-sodium)
- 2 tbsp almond butter (unsweetened)
- 1 medium banana, sliced
- 1/2 tsp chia seeds (optional, for added fiber)
- Drizzle of honey (optional, for added sweetness)

Customizable Options:
- Add cinnamon: Sprinkle 1/4 tsp for added flavor.
- Add fresh berries: For a burst of antioxidants and extra fiber.
- Substitute almond butter: Use peanut butter or any other nut/seed butter.
- Add protein: Include a small handful of chopped nuts or seeds for an extra crunch.

Instructions:

1. Prepare the Tortilla:
 Lay the whole grain tortilla flat on a clean surface.
2. Spread the Almond Butter:
 Evenly spread the almond butter across the surface of the tortilla, leaving a little space at the edges to prevent overflow when rolling.
3. Add the Banana Slices:
 Arrange the banana slices evenly across the almond butter.
4. Garnish with Chia Seeds:
 Sprinkle chia seeds over the banana and almond butter mixture for an added boost of omega-3s and fiber.
5. Optional Drizzle:
 Drizzle a small amount of honey over the filling if desired for extra sweetness.
6. Roll and Serve:
 Gently roll up the tortilla, folding in the sides as you roll. Slice in half and serve.

Nutr. (Per Serving): Calories: 320 | Prot: 8g | Carbs: 45g | Fat: 12g | Fiber: 8g | Chol: 0mg | Na: 120mg | K: 450mg

Whole Grain Waffles with Blueberry Compote

 10 min | 10 min | 4 svgs.

Ingredients:

For the Waffles:
- 1 cup whole wheat flour
- 1/4 cup rolled oats
- 1 tbsp ground flaxseeds
- 1 tsp baking powder
- 1/2 tsp cinnamon
- 1 cup unsweetened almond milk (or other plant-based milk)
- 1 large egg white (or 1 flax egg for a vegan option)
- 1 tbsp olive oil (or melted coconut oil)
- 1 tsp vanilla extract
- 1 tbsp maple syrup (optional, for sweetness)

For the Blueberry Compote:
- 1 cup fresh or frozen blueberries
- 1 tbsp water
- 1 tbsp maple syrup (optional)
- 1/2 tsp lemon zest
- 1/2 tsp vanilla extract

Instructions:

1. Preheat the Waffle Iron:
 Set your waffle iron to medium heat and lightly grease it with non-stick spray.
2. Mix the Dry Ingredients:
 In a large bowl, whisk together the whole wheat flour, rolled oats, ground flaxseeds, baking powder, and cinnamon.
3. Combine Wet Ingredients:
 In a separate bowl, whisk the almond milk, egg white, olive oil, vanilla extract, and maple syrup (if using) until fully combined.
4. Mix Waffle Batter:
 Slowly add the wet ingredients to the dry ingredients, stirring just until combined. Avoid overmixing to keep the waffles light and fluffy.
5. Cook the Waffles:
 Pour 1/4 cup batter into the waffle iron and cook for 3-5 minutes, until golden. Repeat.
6. Prepare the Blueberry Compote:
 While waffles cook, combine blueberries, water, maple syrup (optional), lemon zest, and vanilla in a small saucepan over medium heat. Cook for 5-7 minutes, stirring occasionally, until berries break down into a thick compote.
7. Serve:
 Top each waffle with a generous spoonful of blueberry compote. Optionally, garnish with fresh blueberries, a drizzle of maple syrup, or a sprinkle of nuts for added texture.

Nutr. (Per Serving): Calories: 230 | Prot: 6g | Carbs: 38g | Fat: 7g | Fiber: 7g | Chol: 0mg | Na: 150mg | K: 180mg

Savory Oatmeal with Sautéed Vegetables and Poached Egg

 10 min | 15 min | 1 svgs.

Ingredients:

- 1/2 cup rolled oats
- 1 cup water or low-sodium vegetable broth
- 1 tsp olive oil
- 1/4 cup spinach, fresh
- 1/4 cup mushrooms, sliced
- 1/4 cup cherry tomatoes, halved
- 1 large egg (or egg white for an even lower cholesterol option)
- Salt and pepper to taste
- Fresh herbs (e.g., parsley or chives) for garnish

Customizable Options:
- Add avocado slices for extra healthy fats.
- Top with a sprinkle of feta cheese for added creaminess (optional).
- Use other vegetables like bell peppers, zucchini, or kale.

Instructions:

1. Cook the Oats:
 In a small saucepan, bring water or low-sodium vegetable broth to a boil. Add the rolled oats, reduce the heat, and simmer for 5-7 minutes, stirring occasionally, until the oats are soft and creamy. Season with a pinch of salt and pepper, then set aside.
2. Sauté the Vegetables:
 While the oats cook, heat olive oil in a small skillet over medium heat. Add the mushrooms and sauté for 3-4 minutes until they soften. Add the spinach and cherry tomatoes, sautéing for another 2-3 minutes until the vegetables are wilted and tender. Season with salt and pepper to taste.
3. Poach the Egg:
 In a small saucepan, bring about 2 inches of water to a gentle simmer. Crack the egg into a small bowl, then gently slide it into the water. Poach for about 3-4 minutes, or until the white is set but the yolk remains runny. Remove with a slotted spoon and set aside.
4. Assemble the Bowl:
 Spoon the cooked oatmeal into a bowl, top with the sautéed vegetables, and place the poached egg on top.
5. Garnish and Serve:
 Garnish with fresh herbs, and season with an extra sprinkle of pepper if desired. Serve immediately while warm.

Nutr. (Per Serving): Cl: 280 | Prot: 12g | Carbs: 35g | Fat: 9g | Fiber: 7g | Chol: 180mg (or 0mg if using egg white) | Na: 140mg | K: 450mg

Spinach and Feta Stuffed Whole Wheat Crepes

⏱ 10 min | 🍳 20 min | 🍽 4 svgs.

Ingredients:

For the Crepes:
- 1/2 cup whole wheat flour
- 1 large egg white
- 3/4 cup unsweetened almond milk (or low-fat milk)
- 1/4 cup water
- 1 tbsp olive oil (plus more for cooking)
- Pinch of salt

For the Filling:
- 2 cups fresh spinach, roughly chopped
- 1/3 cup crumbled low-fat feta cheese
- 1 clove garlic, minced
- 1 tsp olive oil
- Freshly ground black pepper to taste
- Fresh herbs (like parsley or dill) for garnish

Instructions:

1. Prepare the Crepe Batter:
 In a large bowl, whisk together the whole wheat flour, egg white, almond milk, water, olive oil, and a pinch of salt until the batter is smooth and free of lumps. Let it rest for about 5 minutes.

2. Cook the Crepes:
 Heat a small amount of olive oil in a non-stick skillet over medium heat. Pour about 1/4 cup of the crepe batter into the skillet, swirling it to evenly coat the bottom. Cook for 1-2 minutes on each side, or until golden brown. Repeat with the remaining batter, setting the cooked crepes aside.

3. Sauté the Spinach Filling:
 In another skillet, heat 1 tsp of olive oil over medium heat. Add the minced garlic and sauté for 30 seconds until fragrant. Add the chopped spinach and cook until wilted, about 2-3 minutes. Remove from heat and stir in the crumbled feta cheese. Season with black pepper to taste.

4. Assemble the Crepes:
 Place a portion of the spinach and feta filling in the center of each crepe. Fold the crepes into quarters or roll them up, depending on your preference.

5. Serve and Garnish:
 Transfer the filled crepes to a plate and garnish with fresh herbs like parsley or dill. Serve warm with a side of mixed greens or a small salad for added freshness.

Nutr. (Per Serving): Cal: 220 | Prot: 9g | Carbs: 25g | Fat: 9g | Fiber: 5g | Chol: 20mg (lower with egg white only) | Na: 310mg | K: 400mg

Egg White and Veggie Breakfast Pizza on Whole Wheat Crust

⏱ 10 min | 🍳 15 min | 🍽 2 svgs.

Ingredients:

For the Crust:
- 1 whole wheat pizza crust (store-bought or homemade, about 10 inches in diameter)

For the Topping:
- 4 large egg whites
- 1/2 cup spinach, roughly chopped
- 1/4 cup bell peppers, thinly sliced
- 1/4 cup cherry tomatoes, halved
- 1/4 cup low-fat mozzarella cheese, shredded (optional)
- 1 tsp olive oil
- 1/4 tsp garlic powder
- Salt and pepper to taste
- Fresh herbs (e.g., basil or parsley) for garnish

Instructions:

1. Preheat the Oven:
 Preheat your oven to 400°F (200°C). If using a store-bought whole wheat pizza crust, place it on a baking sheet or pizza stone.

2. Prepare the Egg Whites:
 In a non-stick skillet, heat 1 tsp of olive oil over medium heat. Add the spinach, bell peppers, and cherry tomatoes. Sauté for 3-4 minutes until the vegetables are softened. Add the egg whites, season with garlic powder, salt, and pepper, and cook until the egg whites are just set, stirring occasionally.

3. Assemble the Pizza:
 Spread the sautéed egg whites and vegetables evenly over the whole wheat crust. Sprinkle the low-fat mozzarella cheese (if using) over the top.

4. Bake the Pizza:
 Transfer the pizza to the preheated oven and bake for 8-10 minutes, or until the crust is golden and crisp, and the cheese is melted (if added).

5. Garnish and Serve:
 Remove the pizza from the oven, garnish with fresh herbs like basil or parsley, and slice into wedges. Serve immediately.

Nutr. (Per Serving): Calories: 250 | Prot: 18g | Carbs: 28g | Fat: 8g | Fiber: 6g | Chol: 0mg | Na: 320mg | K: 420mg

SNACKS AND APPETIZERS

Roasted Chickpeas with Smoked Paprika and Garlic

🕐 5 min 🍳 30 min 🔔 4 svgs.

Ingredients:

- 1 can (15 oz) chickpeas, drained and rinsed
- 1 tbsp olive oil
- 1 tsp smoked paprika
- 1/2 tsp garlic powder
- 1/4 tsp salt
- Freshly ground black pepper to taste
- Optional garnish: Fresh herbs (e.g., parsley), lemon wedges

Customizable Options:
- Add cayenne pepper for a spicier kick.
- Use other spices like cumin or rosemary for different flavor profiles.
- Add a squeeze of lemon juice after roasting for a burst of freshness.

Instructions:

1.Preheat the Oven:
 Preheat your oven to 400°F (200°C). Line a baking sheet with parchment paper or lightly grease it with olive oil.

2.Dry the Chickpeas:
 Pat the chickpeas dry with a clean kitchen towel or paper towel. Removing excess moisture helps them roast to a crispier texture.

3. Season the Chickpeas:
 In a large bowl, toss the chickpeas with olive oil, smoked paprika, garlic powder, salt, and pepper. Make sure they are evenly coated with the spices.

4.Roast the Chickpeas:
 Spread the seasoned chickpeas in a single layer on the prepared baking sheet. Roast in the preheated oven for 30-35 minutes, stirring halfway through, until they are golden and crispy.

5.Cool and Serve:
 Let the chickpeas cool for a few minutes to allow them to crisp up further. Garnish with fresh herbs and a squeeze of lemon juice, if desired, and serve warm or at room temperature.

Nutr. (Per Serving): Calories: 140 | Prot: 6g | Carbs: 18g | Fat: 5g | Fiber: 6g | Chol: 0mg | Na: 190mg | K: 200mg

Stuffed Mini Bell Peppers with Quinoa and Herbs

🕐 10 min 🍳 20 min 🔔 4 svgs.

Ingredients:

- 12 mini bell peppers, halved and seeds removed
- 1/2 cup quinoa, rinsed and drained
- 1 cup vegetable broth (low-sodium)
- 1 tbsp olive oil
- 1/4 cup red onion, finely diced
- 1/4 cup cherry tomatoes, diced
- 1/4 cup fresh parsley, chopped
- 1 tbsp fresh basil, chopped
- 1 garlic clove, minced
- 1/4 tsp black pepper
- Salt to taste
- Lemon wedges (optional, for serving)

Customizable Options:
- Add cheese: Crumble a little low-fat feta or goat cheese for added creaminess.
- Add nuts: Sprinkle toasted pine nuts or sunflower seeds for added crunch.
- Use different herbs: Try cilantro or dill for a different flavor profile.

Instructions:

1.Cook the Quinoa:
 In a small saucepan, cook rinsed quinoa with vegetable broth for 12-15 minutes, until tender and liquid is absorbed. Fluff with a fork and set aside.

2.Prepare the Peppers:
 Preheat oven to 375°F (190°C). Halve and deseed mini bell peppers. Drizzle with 1/2 tbsp olive oil and place cut-side up on a baking sheet.

3.Prepare the Quinoa Filling:
 In a skillet, heat 1/2 tbsp olive oil over medium heat. Sauté onion and garlic for 2-3 minutes. Add tomatoes and cooked quinoa. Stir in parsley, basil, salt, and pepper.

4.Stuff the Peppers:
 Spoon the quinoa mixture into each mini bell pepper half, filling them generously. Place the stuffed peppers back on the baking sheet.

5.Bake the Peppers:
 Bake in the preheated oven for 10-12 minutes until the peppers are tender but still hold their shape.

6.Serve:
 Remove the stuffed peppers from the oven, garnish with extra fresh herbs, and serve warm with a squeeze of lemon for added brightness.

Nutr. (Per Serving): Calories: 160 | Prot: 4g | Carbs: 20g | Fat: 6g | Fiber: 4g | Chol: 0mg | Na: 150mg | K: 350mg

Ingredients:

For the Zucchini Fries:
- 2 medium zucchini, cut into fry-like strips
- 1/2 cup whole wheat breadcrumbs
- 1/4 cup grated Parmesan cheese (optional for flavor)
- 1 tsp garlic powder
- 1 tsp smoked paprika
- 2 egg whites, lightly beaten
- 1/4 tsp salt
- Freshly ground black pepper to taste

For the Lemon Aioli:
- 1/4 cup low-fat Greek yogurt
- 1 tbsp olive oil mayonnaise (or regular low-fat mayo)
- 1 tsp lemon zest
- 1 tbsp lemon juice
- 1 garlic clove, minced
- Salt and pepper to taste

Instructions:

1. Preheat the Oven:
 Preheat your oven to 400°F (200°C). Line a baking sheet with parchment paper or lightly grease with olive oil spray.
2. Prepare the Zucchini Fries:
 In a bowl, combine the whole wheat breadcrumbs, Parmesan cheese (if using), garlic powder, smoked paprika, salt, and pepper. Set aside.
3. Coat the Zucchini:
 Dip each zucchini strip into the beaten egg whites, then coat with the breadcrumb mixture. Place the coated zucchini on the prepared baking sheet in a single layer.
4. Bake the Zucchini Fries:

 Bake in the preheated oven for 20-25 minutes, flipping halfway through, until the fries are golden brown and crispy.
5. Prepare the Lemon Aioli:
 While the zucchini fries are baking, whisk together the Greek yogurt, olive oil mayonnaise, lemon zest, lemon juice, and minced garlic in a small bowl. Season with salt and pepper to taste.
6. Serve:
 Once the zucchini fries are ready, serve them warm with the lemon aioli on the side for dipping. Garnish with fresh herbs if desired.

Nutr. (Per Serving): Calories: 130 | Prot: 7g | Carbs: 12g | Fat: 6g | Fiber: 3g | Chol: 5mg (0mg w/o Parmesan) | Na: 250mg | K: 320mg

Ingredients:

For the Sweet Potato Chips:
- 2 medium sweet potatoes, thinly sliced (about 1/8 inch thick)
- 1 tbsp olive oil
- 1/2 tsp smoked paprika (optional)
- 1/2 tsp garlic powder
- Salt and pepper to taste

For the Cilantro Lime Yogurt Dip:
- 1/2 cup low-fat Greek yogurt
- 1 tbsp lime juice
- 1 tsp lime zest
- 1 tbsp fresh cilantro, finely chopped
- 1 garlic clove, minced
- Salt and pepper to taste

Customizable Options:
- Add spice: Sprinkle chili powder or cayenne for a spicy version.
- Add crunch: Use nutritional yeast on the chips for extra flavor.

Instructions:

1. Preheat the Oven:
 Preheat your oven to 375°F (190°C) and line two baking sheets with parchment paper.
2. Prepare the Sweet Potatoes:
 In a large bowl, toss the thinly sliced sweet potatoes with olive oil, smoked paprika, garlic powder, salt, and pepper until evenly coated.
3. Arrange and Bake:
 Arrange the sweet potato slices in a single layer on the prepared baking sheets, ensuring they don't overlap. Bake for 25-30 minutes, flipping halfway through, until the chips are golden and crispy.

4. Make the Cilantro Lime Yogurt Dip:
 While the chips are baking, whisk together the Greek yogurt, lime juice, lime zest, cilantro, minced garlic, salt, and pepper in a small bowl. Adjust seasoning to taste.
5. Serve:
 Once the chips are crispy, remove them from the oven and let them cool slightly. Serve the chips warm or at room temperature with the cilantro lime yogurt dip on the side.

Nutr. (Per Serving): Calories: 130 | Prot: 3g | Carbs: 22g | Fat: 4g | Fiber: 4g | Chol: 0mg | Na: 150mg | K: 330mg

Ingredients:

For the Guacamole:
- 2 ripe avocados
- 1 small tomato, diced
- 1/4 cup red onion, finely chopped
- 1 tbsp fresh cilantro, chopped
- 1 garlic clove, minced
- 1 tbsp lime juice
- Salt and pepper to taste

For the Veggie Sticks:
- 1 large carrot, peeled and cut into sticks
- 1 bell pepper, cut into strips
- 1 cucumber, sliced into sticks
- 2 celery stalks, cut into sticks

Customizable Options:
- Add spice: Include a pinch of cayenne pepper or diced jalapeño for extra heat.
- Swap veggies: Use zucchini or cherry tomatoes as alternative veggie sticks.

Instructions:

1. Prepare the Guacamole:

In a medium bowl, mash the ripe avocados until smooth but still slightly chunky. Add the diced tomato, chopped red onion, cilantro, minced garlic, and lime juice. Season with salt and pepper to taste. Stir until well combined.

2. Prepare the Veggie Sticks:

While the guacamole is coming together, slice the carrots, bell peppers, cucumbers, and celery into sticks or strips.

3. Serve:

Place the guacamole in a serving bowl, and arrange the fresh veggie sticks around it. Garnish the guacamole with extra cilantro or a squeeze of lime if desired.

Nutr. (Per Serving): Calories: 150 | Prot: 2g | Carbs: 14g | Fat: 11g | Fiber: 7g | Chol: 0mg | Na: 80mg | K: 500mg

Ingredients:

- 12 large button or cremini mushrooms, stems removed
- 1/2 cup cooked lentils
- 1/4 cup whole wheat breadcrumbs
- 1 garlic clove, minced
- 2 tbsp fresh parsley, chopped (plus more for garnish)
- 1 tbsp fresh basil, chopped
- 1 tsp olive oil (plus more for greasing the pan)
- 1 tbsp lemon juice
- Salt and pepper to taste

Customizable Options:
- Add cheese: Sprinkle a little low-fat Parmesan or nutritional yeast for extra flavor.
- Swap herbs: Use thyme or cilantro for a different flavor profile.

Instructions:

1. Preheat the Oven:

Preheat your oven to 375°F (190°C). Lightly grease a baking sheet or baking dish with olive oil.

2. Prepare the Mushroom Caps:

Clean the mushrooms and carefully remove the stems. Set the mushroom caps aside. Finely chop the mushroom stems to include in the filling.

3. Make the Filling:

In a medium skillet, heat 1 tsp of olive oil over medium heat. Add the minced garlic and chopped mushroom stems, sautéing for 2-3 minutes until soft. Stir in the cooked lentils, breadcrumbs, parsley, basil, lemon juice, salt, and pepper. Cook for another 2 minutes, stirring to combine.

4. Stuff the Mushrooms:

Spoon the lentil and herb mixture into the mushroom caps, filling each generously. Place the stuffed mushrooms on the prepared baking sheet.

5. Bake the Mushrooms:

Bake for 20-25 minutes, or until the mushrooms are tender and the filling is golden brown on top.

6. Garnish and Serve:

Remove from the oven and garnish with fresh parsley. Serve warm as a side dish or appetizer.

Nutr. (Per Serving): Calories: 110 | Prot: 6g | Carbs: 14g | Fat: 3g | Fiber: 5g | Chol: 0mg | Na: 160mg | K: 350mg

Spicy Roasted Cauliflower Bites

Ingredients:

- 1 medium head of cauliflower, cut into bite-sized florets
- 2 tbsp olive oil
- 1 tsp smoked paprika
- 1 tsp chili powder
- 1/2 tsp garlic powder
- 1/4 tsp cumin
- 1/4 tsp cayenne pepper (optional, for extra heat)
- Salt and freshly ground black pepper to taste

- Fresh parsley (for garnish, optional)

Customizable Options:
- Add a squeeze of lemon juice after roasting for brightness.
- Top with sesame seeds for a crunchy finish.

Instructions:

1. Preheat the Oven:
 Preheat your oven to 425°F (220°C). Line a baking sheet with parchment paper or lightly grease it with olive oil.

2. Season the Cauliflower:
 In a large bowl, toss the cauliflower florets with olive oil, smoked paprika, chili powder, garlic powder, cumin, cayenne pepper, salt, and pepper. Ensure that the florets are evenly coated with the seasoning.

3. Roast the Cauliflower:
 Spread the seasoned cauliflower in a single layer on the prepared baking sheet. Roast in the preheated oven for 25-30 minutes, flipping halfway through, until the cauliflower is golden brown and slightly charred around the edges.

4. Garnish and Serve:
 Once roasted, remove the cauliflower from the oven and garnish with fresh parsley if desired. Serve warm as a snack or side dish.

Nutr. (Per Serving): Calories: 110 | Prot: 3g | Carbs: 10g | Fat: 7g | Fiber: 4g | Chol: 0mg | Na: 200mg | K: 450mg

Avocado and Black Bean Salsa with Baked Tortilla Chips

Ingredients:

For the Salsa:
- 1 large avocado, diced
- 1 cup canned black beans, drained and rinsed
- 1/2 cup corn kernels (fresh or canned, drained)
- 1/2 cup cherry tomatoes, diced
- 1/4 cup red onion, finely chopped
- 2 tbsp fresh cilantro, chopped
- 1 tbsp lime juice
- 1/2 tsp ground cumin

- Salt and pepper to taste

For the Baked Tortilla Chips:
- 4 whole wheat tortillas
- 1 tbsp olive oil
- 1/2 tsp chili powder (optional)
- 1/4 tsp garlic powder
- Salt to taste

Instructions:

1. Prepare the Salsa:
 In a medium bowl, combine the diced avocado, black beans, corn, tomatoes, red onion, and cilantro. Add the lime juice, ground cumin, salt, and pepper. Toss gently to combine. Adjust seasoning to taste.

2. Make the Baked Tortilla Chips:
 Preheat the oven to 350°F (180°C). Brush both sides of the whole wheat tortillas with olive oil. Cut each tortilla into 6 wedges and place them on a baking sheet. Sprinkle with chili powder, garlic powder, and a pinch of salt. Bake for 10-15 minutes, flipping halfway through, until golden and crispy.

3. Serve:
 Serve the fresh salsa with the baked tortilla chips on the side. Garnish with extra cilantro or a squeeze of lime if desired.

Nutr. (Per Serving): Calories: 220 | Prot: 6g | Carbs: 32g | Fat: 10g | Fiber: 9g | Chol: 0mg | Na: 250mg | K: 500mg

Tomato Basil Bruschetta on Whole Wheat Baguette

 10 min · 5 min · 4 svgs.

Ingredients:

- 1 whole wheat baguette, sliced into 12 slices
- 2 medium tomatoes, diced
- 1/4 cup fresh basil, chopped
- 1 garlic clove, minced
- 1 tbsp extra virgin olive oil
- 1 tsp balsamic vinegar (optional)
- Salt and pepper to taste

Customizable Options:

- Add red pepper flakes for a little heat.
- Top with low-fat mozzarella for a cheesy variation.
- Use cherry tomatoes for a sweeter flavor.

Instructions:

1. Prepare the Baguette:

Preheat your oven to 375°F (190°C). Arrange the whole wheat baguette slices on a baking sheet. Lightly brush each slice with olive oil. Toast in the oven for about 5 minutes, until golden and crisp.

2. Prepare the Tomato Mixture:

In a medium bowl, combine the diced tomatoes, chopped basil, minced garlic, and a drizzle of olive oil. Add balsamic vinegar (if using) and season with salt and pepper to taste.

3. Assemble the Bruschetta:

Once the baguette slices are toasted, remove them from the oven and let them cool slightly. Spoon the tomato mixture onto each slice of baguette, making sure to spread it evenly.

4. Serve:

Arrange the bruschetta on a serving platter and garnish with extra basil or a drizzle of balsamic glaze if desired. Serve immediately.

Nutr. (Per Serving): Calories: 140 | Prot: 4g | Carbs: 22g | Fat: 5g | Fiber: 4g | Chol: 0mg | Na: 150mg | K: 240mg

Roasted Red Pepper Hummus with Whole Wheat Pita Bread

 10 min · 10 min · 4 svgs.

Ingredients:

For the Roasted Red Pepper Hummus:

- 1 can (15 oz) chickpeas, drained and rinsed
- 1/2 cup roasted red peppers, roughly chopped
- 2 tbsp tahini
- 2 tbsp lemon juice
- 1 garlic clove, minced
- 2 tbsp extra virgin olive oil (plus more for drizzling)
- 1/2 tsp cumin
- Salt and pepper to taste
- Fresh herbs for garnish (optional)

For the Pita Bread:

- 2 whole wheat pita breads, cut into wedges
- 1 tbsp olive oil (for brushing)
- Salt (optional, for seasoning)

Instructions:

1. Prepare the Hummus:

In a food processor, combine the chickpeas, roasted red peppers, tahini, lemon juice, garlic, olive oil, and cumin. Blend until smooth, adding 1-2 tbsp of water if needed to achieve the desired consistency. Season with salt and pepper to taste.

2. Toast the Pita Bread:

Preheat the oven to 350°F (175°C). Brush the whole wheat pita wedges with olive oil and sprinkle lightly with salt if desired. Arrange on a baking sheet and bake for 8-10 minutes, or until golden and crisp.

3. Serve:

Spoon the hummus into a serving bowl and drizzle with a little extra olive oil. Garnish with fresh herbs if desired. Arrange the toasted pita wedges around the hummus and serve immediately.

Nutr. (Per Serving): Calories: 230 | Prot: 7g | Carbs: 25g | Fat: 10g | Fiber: 6g | Chol: 0mg | Na: 280mg | K: 350mg

Ingredients:

- For the Falafel Bites:
- 1 can (15 oz) chickpeas, drained and rinsed
- 1/4 cup fresh parsley, chopped
- 1/4 cup fresh cilantro, chopped
- 1 small onion, finely chopped
- 2 garlic cloves, minced
- 1 tsp cumin
- 1 tsp ground coriander
- 1/4 tsp cayenne pepper (optional)
- 1/2 tsp baking powder
- 2 tbsp whole wheat flour
- 1 tbsp olive oil
- Salt and pepper to taste

For the Cucumber Yogurt Sauce:
- 1/2 cup low-fat Greek yogurt
- 1/4 cucumber, finely grated
- 1 tbsp fresh lemon juice
- 1 garlic clove, minced
- 1 tbsp fresh dill, chopped (optional)
- Salt and pepper to taste

Instructions:

1. Prepare the Falafel Mixture:
In a food processor, combine the chickpeas, parsley, cilantro, onion, garlic, cumin, ground coriander, baking powder, and olive oil. Pulse until the mixture is well combined but still slightly chunky. Add the whole wheat flour and pulse again to combine. Season with salt and pepper.

2. Form the Falafel Bites:
Preheat your oven to 400°F (200°C) and line a baking sheet with parchment paper. Use a spoon or your hands to form the falafel mixture into small bite-sized balls and place them on the baking sheet.

3. Bake the Falafel Bites:
Lightly brush the falafel bites with a little olive oil and bake for 20-25 minutes, flipping halfway through, until they are golden and crispy on the outside.

4. Prepare the Cucumber Yogurt Sauce:
While the falafel bites are baking, mix together the Greek yogurt, grated cucumber, lemon juice, minced garlic, and dill (if using) in a small bowl. Season with salt and pepper to taste.

5. Serve:
Serve the warm falafel bites with the cucumber yogurt sauce on the side for dipping. Garnish with extra parsley or cilantro if desired.

Nutr. (Per Serving): Calories: 180 | Prot: 7g | Carbs: 25g | Fat: 6g | Fiber: 6g | Chol: 0mg | Na: 280mg | K: 320mg

Ingredients:

For the Quinoa Patties:
- 1 cup cooked quinoa
- 1/4 cup whole wheat breadcrumbs
- 1/4 cup grated carrots
- 2 tbsp finely chopped red onion
- 1 tbsp fresh parsley, chopped
- 1 tbsp fresh cilantro, chopped
- 1 garlic clove, minced
- 1 large egg white
- 1 tsp cumin
- 1 tbsp olive oil (for cooking)
- Salt and pepper to taste

For the Fresh Salsa:
- 2 medium tomatoes, diced
- 1/4 cup red onion, finely diced
- 1 tbsp fresh cilantro, chopped
- 1 tbsp lime juice
- Salt and pepper to taste

Instructions:

1. Prepare the Quinoa Patties:
In a large bowl, combine the cooked quinoa, breadcrumbs, grated carrots, red onion, parsley, cilantro, minced garlic, and cumin. Add the egg white and season with salt and pepper. Mix until everything is well combined and holds together.

2. Form the Patties:
Shape the mixture into small patties (about 2 inches in diameter). You should get about 12 mini patties.

3. Cook the Patties:
Heat olive oil in a non-stick skillet over medium heat. Cook the patties for about 3-4 minutes on each side until they are golden and crispy. Transfer to a paper towel-lined plate to drain any excess oil.

4. Prepare the Fresh Salsa:
In a small bowl, combine the diced tomatoes, red onion, cilantro, and lime juice. Season with salt and pepper. Mix well and set aside.

5. Serve:
Serve the mini quinoa patties warm with the fresh salsa on the side. Garnish with extra cilantro if desired.

Nutr. (Per Serving): Calories: 180 | Prot: 6g | Carbs: 25g | Fat: 7g | Fiber: 5g | Chol: 0mg | Na: 220mg | K: 350mg

Ingredients:

For the Filling:
- 2 cups fresh spinach, chopped
- 1/2 cup vegan feta cheese, crumbled
- 1 garlic clove, minced
- 2 tbsp fresh dill, chopped
- 2 tbsp fresh parsley, chopped
- 1 tbsp olive oil
- Salt and pepper to taste

For the Phyllo Rolls:
- 8 sheets of phyllo dough (thawed if frozen)
- 2 tbsp olive oil (for brushing)

Instructions:

1.Prepare the Filling:

In a medium skillet, heat 1 tbsp olive oil over medium heat. Add the minced garlic and sauté for 1-2 minutes until fragrant. Add the chopped spinach and cook for 3-4 minutes until wilted. Remove from heat and stir in the vegan feta, dill, and parsley. Season with salt and pepper to taste. Let the mixture cool slightly.

2.Prepare the Phyllo Dough:

Preheat oven to 375°F (190°C). Lay out a sheet of phyllo dough, brush with olive oil, and repeat until you have four sheets stacked.

3. Assemble the Rolls:

3. Assemble the Rolls:

Cut stacked phyllo into four rectangles. Place filling on one end of each and roll up tightly. Repeat for remaining sheets.

4.Bake the Phyllo Rolls:

Place the rolls on a baking sheet lined with parchment paper. Brush the tops of the rolls with a little more olive oil. Bake in the preheated oven for 20-25 minutes, or until the rolls are golden and crispy.

5. Serve:

Remove from the oven and allow the rolls to cool for a few minutes before serving. Garnish with extra fresh herbs if desired.

Nutr. (Per Serving): Calories: 200 | Prot: 6g | Carbs: 20g | Fat: 12g | Fiber: 3g | Chol: 0mg | Na: 290mg | K: 320mg

Ingredients:

For the Baked Eggplant Rounds:
- 1 medium eggplant, sliced into 1/2-inch rounds
- 1/2 cup whole wheat breadcrumbs
- 1/4 cup grated Parmesan cheese (optional)
- 1/2 tsp garlic powder
- 1/2 tsp smoked paprika
- 1/4 tsp black pepper
- 1 large egg white, lightly beaten
- 2 tbsp olive oil (for brushing)

For the Marinara Dipping Sauce:
- 1 cup marinara sauce (store-bought or homemade)
- 1 garlic clove, minced
- 1 tbsp fresh basil, chopped (optional)
- 1 tsp olive oil
- Salt and pepper to taste

Instructions:

1.Preheat the Oven:

Preheat your oven to 400°F (200°C). Line a baking sheet with parchment paper or lightly grease it with olive oil.

2.Prepare the Eggplant Rounds:

In a bowl, combine the breadcrumbs, Parmesan cheese (if using), garlic powder, smoked paprika, and black pepper. Set aside.

3.Coat the Eggplant:

Dip each eggplant round into the beaten egg white, then coat with the breadcrumb mixture. Press the coating onto the eggplant to ensure it sticks well.

4.Bake the Eggplant Rounds:

Arrange the coated eggplant rounds on the prepared baking sheet. Lightly brush the tops with olive oil. Bake for 20-25 minutes, flipping halfway through, until golden and crispy.

5. Prepare the Marinara Sauce:

While the eggplant is baking, heat 1 tsp olive oil in a small saucepan over medium heat. Add the minced garlic and sauté for 1 minute. Stir in the marinara sauce, season with salt and pepper, and simmer for 5 minutes. Add fresh basil if desired.

6.Serve:

Once the eggplant rounds are done, serve them warm with the marinara sauce on the side for dipping.

Nutr. (Per Serving): Calories: 180 | Prot: 5g | Carbs: 20g | Fat: 8g | Fiber: 6g | Chol: 0mg | Na: 250mg | K: 450mg

Baked Polenta Bites with Tomato and Olive Tapenade

Ingredients:

For the Polenta Bites:
- 1 cup polenta (cornmeal)
- 3 cups water
- 1/4 tsp salt
- 1 tbsp olive oil (for baking)
- 1/4 cup grated Parmesan (optional for flavor)

For the Tomato and Olive Tapenade:
- 1/2 cup cherry tomatoes, finely chopped
- 1/4 cup Kalamata olives, pitted and chopped
- 1 tbsp capers, drained
- 1 tbsp fresh parsley, chopped
- 1 tbsp olive oil
- 1 tsp balsamic vinegar
- 1 garlic clove, minced
- Salt and pepper to taste

Instructions:

1.Prepare the Polenta:
 In a medium saucepan, bring 3 cups of water and 1/4 tsp salt to a boil. Gradually whisk in the polenta and reduce the heat to low. Cook, stirring frequently, for about 10-15 minutes, until the mixture thickens and pulls away from the sides of the pan.

2.Cool and Set the Polenta:
 Once the polenta is cooked, spread it evenly onto a baking dish or tray to a thickness of about 1/2 inch. Allow it to cool and set for about 15 minutes.

3.Cut and Bake the Polenta Bites:
 Preheat your oven to 400°F (200°C). Once the polenta is set, cut it into small bite-sized squares or rounds. Place the pieces on a greased or parchment-lined baking sheet, brush lightly with olive oil, and bake for 15-20 minutes, flipping halfway through, until golden and crispy.

4.Prepare the Tomato and Olive Tapenade:
 In a small bowl, combine the chopped tomatoes, Kalamata olives, capers, fresh parsley, minced garlic, olive oil, and balsamic vinegar. Season with salt and pepper to taste.

5.Assemble and Serve:
 Once the polenta bites are baked and crispy, top each piece with a spoonful of the tomato and olive tapenade. Garnish with extra parsley if desired and serve warm.

Nutr. (Per Serving): Calories: 180 | Prot: 4g | Carbs: 22g | Fat: 8g | Fiber: 3g | Chol: 0mg | Na: 220mg | K: 230mg

Caprese Skewers with Balsamic Drizzle

Ingredients:

Ingredients:
- 16 cherry tomatoes
- 16 fresh basil leaves
- 16 mini mozzarella balls (or vegan mozzarella for a cholesterol-free option)
- 2 tbsp balsamic glaze
- 1 tbsp extra virgin olive oil (optional)
- Salt and pepper to taste

16 small skewers or toothpicks

For the Marinara Dipping Sauce:
- 1 cup marinara sauce (store-bought or homemade)
- 1 garlic clove, minced
- 1 tbsp fresh basil, chopped (optional)
- 1 tsp olive oil
- Salt and pepper to taste

Instructions:

1.Assemble the Skewers:
 Thread each skewer with one cherry tomato, one basil leaf, and one mini mozzarella ball. Repeat until all skewers are assembled.

2.Drizzle with Balsamic Glaze:
 Arrange the skewers on a serving platter. Drizzle the skewers with balsamic glaze and olive oil (if using). Season with a light sprinkle of salt and pepper.

3.Serve:
 Serve the skewers immediately, garnished with extra basil leaves if desired.

Nutr.(Per Serving): Cal: 120 | Prot: 6g | Carbs: 5g | Fat: 8g | Fiber: 1g | Chol: 15mg (or 0mg with vegan mozzarella) | Na: 150mg | K: 250mg

Quinoa and Black Bean Power Salad

⏱ 15 min | 🍳 15 min | 🛎 4 svgs.

Ingredients:

For the Salad:
- 1 cup quinoa, rinsed
- 1 can (15 oz) black beans, drained and rinsed
- 1/2 cup corn kernels (fresh or canned)
- 1/2 cup cherry tomatoes, halved
- 1/2 cup bell peppers, diced (red, yellow, or green)
- 1/4 cup red onion, finely chopped
- 1/4 cup fresh cilantro, chopped

For the Dressing:
- 2 tbsp extra virgin olive oil
- 2 tbsp lime juice
- 1 tsp lime zest
- 1 garlic clove, minced
- 1 tsp ground cumin
- Salt and pepper to taste

Instructions:

1.Cook the Quinoa:

In a medium saucepan, bring 2 cups of water and the rinsed quinoa to a boil. Reduce the heat to low, cover, and simmer for about 15 minutes, or until the quinoa has absorbed the water. Remove from heat and fluff with a fork. Set aside to cool.

2.Prepare the Dressing:

In a small bowl, whisk together the olive oil, lime juice, lime zest, minced garlic, ground cumin, and a pinch of salt and pepper.

3.Assemble the Salad:

In a large bowl, combine the cooked quinoa, black beans, corn, cherry tomatoes, bell peppers, red onion, and cilantro. Pour the dressing over the salad and toss to coat all the ingredients evenly.

4.Serve:

Serve the salad immediately, or chill it in the refrigerator for 20 minutes to allow the flavors to blend. Garnish with extra cilantro and lime wedges if desired.

Nutr. (Per Serving): Calories: 280 | Prot: 9g | Carbs: 42g | Fat: 9g | Fiber: 8g | Chol: 0mg | Na: 300mg | K: 550mg

Spinach and Strawberry Salad with Balsamic Vinaigrette

⏱ 10 min | 🍳 0 min | 🛎 4 svgs.

Ingredients:

For the Salad:
- 4 cups baby spinach leaves, washed
- 1 cup strawberries, hulled and sliced
- 1/4 cup slivered almonds (or walnuts)
- 1/4 small red onion, thinly sliced (optional)

For the Balsamic Vinaigrette:
- 2 tbsp balsamic vinegar
- 1 tbsp extra virgin olive oil
- 1 tsp Dijon mustard
- 1 tsp honey (optional)
- Salt and pepper, to taste

Instructions:

1.Prepare the Vinaigrette:

In a small bowl, whisk together the balsamic vinegar, olive oil, Dijon mustard, honey, salt, and pepper until well combined.

2.Assemble the Salad:

In a large salad bowl, combine the baby spinach, sliced strawberries, slivered almonds, and red onion (if using). Toss gently to combine.

3.Dress the Salad:

Drizzle the balsamic vinaigrette over the salad just before serving, and toss lightly to coat the ingredients.

4.Serve:

Serve the salad immediately as a refreshing side dish or light meal.

Nutr. (Per Serving): Calories: 120 | Prot: 2g | Carbs: 8g | Fat: 8g | Fiber: 3g | Chol: 0mg | Na: 50mg | K: 300mg

Grilled Vegetable Skewers with Herb Dressing

Ingredients:

For the Skewers:
- 1 red bell pepper, cut into 1-inch squares
- 1 yellow bell pepper, cut into 1-inch squares
- 1 zucchini, sliced into rounds
- 1 red onion, cut into wedges
- 12 cherry tomatoes
- 2 tbsp olive oil
- Salt and pepper to taste

For the Herb Dressing:
- 2 tbsp extra virgin olive oil
- 1 tbsp fresh lemon juice
- 1 tbsp fresh parsley, chopped
- 1 tbsp fresh basil, chopped
- 1 garlic clove, minced
- Salt and pepper to taste

Instructions:

1. Prepare the Vegetables:
Thread the bell peppers, zucchini, red onion, and cherry tomatoes onto skewers, alternating the vegetables for color and balance.

2. Season and Grill the Skewers:
Brush the vegetable skewers with olive oil and season with salt and pepper. Preheat a grill or grill pan over medium heat. Grill the skewers for 8-10 minutes, turning occasionally, until the vegetables are tender and slightly charred.

3. Make the Herb Dressing:
In a small bowl, whisk together the extra virgin olive oil, lemon juice, fresh parsley, basil, and minced garlic. Season with salt and pepper to taste.

4. Serve the Skewers:
Once the skewers are done, drizzle the herb dressing over the grilled vegetables and serve immediately.

Nutr. (Per Serving): Calories: 150 | Prot: 3g | Carbs: 10g | Fat: 11g | Fiber: 3g | Chol: 0mg | Na: 150mg | K: 350mg

Kale and Apple Slaw with Honey Mustard Dressing

Ingredients:

For the Slaw:
- 4 cups kale, finely chopped
- 1 large apple, thinly sliced (any variety, preferably sweet)
- 1/2 cup shredded carrots
- 1/4 cup red cabbage, shredded (optional for color)
- 1/4 cup slivered almonds (optional for crunch)

For the Honey Mustard Dressing:
- 2 tbsp Dijon mustard
- 1 tbsp honey (or maple syrup for vegan option)
- 1 tbsp apple cider vinegar
- 2 tbsp extra virgin olive oil
- Salt and pepper to taste

Instructions:

1. Prepare the Vegetables:
In a large bowl, combine the chopped kale, thinly sliced apple, shredded carrots, and red cabbage (if using). Toss gently to combine.

2. Make the Honey Mustard Dressing:
In a small bowl, whisk together the Dijon mustard, honey, apple cider vinegar, olive oil, salt, and pepper until well combined.

3. Dress the Slaw:
Pour the honey mustard dressing over the slaw and toss until all the ingredients are evenly coated.

4. Optional Garnishes:
Sprinkle the slivered almonds over the top for added crunch, or add dried cranberries for extra sweetness if desired.

5. Serve:
Serve the slaw immediately or chill for 10 minutes to allow the flavors to blend.

Nutr. (Per Serving): Calories: 150 | Prot: 3g | Carbs: 18g | Fat: 8g | Fiber: 4g | Chol: 0mg | Na: 120mg | K: 300mg

⏱ 10 min   🍳 40 min   🍽 4 svgs.

Ingredients:

For the Salad:
- 4 medium beets, peeled and cut into wedges
- 4 cups arugula, washed
- 1/4 cup walnuts, toasted (optional)
- 1/4 cup feta cheese, crumbled (optional)

For the Citrus Dressing:
- 2 tbsp fresh orange juice
- 1 tbsp fresh lemon juice
- 1 tbsp extra virgin olive oil
- 1 tsp Dijon mustard
- 1 tsp honey (or maple syrup for vegan option)
- Salt and pepper, to taste

Instructions:

1.Roast the Beets:
 Preheat your oven to 400°F (200°C). Toss the beet wedges in a little olive oil, and spread them on a baking sheet. Roast for 35-40 minutes, turning halfway through, until tender and caramelized. Let cool slightly.

2.Prepare the Dressing:
 In a small bowl, whisk together the orange juice, lemon juice, olive oil, Dijon mustard, honey, salt, and pepper until well combined.

3.Assemble the Salad:
 In a large salad bowl, combine the arugula, roasted beets, and toasted walnuts (if using). Drizzle the citrus dressing over the salad and toss gently to combine.

4.Optional Garnishes:
 Top the salad with crumbled feta for added creaminess, or keep it vegan by leaving it out.

5.Serve:
 Serve the salad immediately as a light main course or as a side dish.

Nutr. (Per Serving): Calories: 180 | Prot: 4g | Carbs: 20g | Fat: 10g | Fiber: 5g | Chol: 0mg | Na: 150mg | K: 400mg

⏱ 10 min   🍳 0 min   🍽 4 svgs.

Ingredients:

- 2 ripe avocados, diced
- 2 medium tomatoes, diced
- 1/4 cup red onion, finely chopped
- 2 tbsp fresh cilantro, chopped
- 1 tbsp lime juice
- Salt and pepper, to taste

Instructions:

1.Prepare the Ingredients:
 In a medium bowl, combine the diced avocado, tomatoes, red onion, and cilantro.

2.Add the Dressing:
 Drizzle the lime juice over the ingredients and season with salt and pepper to taste. Toss gently to combine, ensuring the avocado stays in chunks.

3.Serve:
 Serve immediately as a side dish or refrigerate for up to 1 hour to allow the flavors to meld together.

Nutr. (Per Serving): Calories: 120 | Prot: 2g | Carbs: 9g | Fat: 9g | Fiber: 5g | Chol: 0mg | Na: 90mg | K: 350mg

Ingredients:

For the Salad:
- 2 medium cucumbers, thinly sliced (use a mandoline for uniform slices)
- 1/2 small red onion, thinly sliced
- 1/4 cup radishes, thinly sliced (optional for extra crunch and color)
- 2 tbsp fresh dill, chopped

For the Greek Yogurt Dill Dressing:
- 1/4 cup plain Greek yogurt (low-fat or fat-free)
- 1 tbsp extra virgin olive oil
- 1 tbsp lemon juice
- 1 tsp Dijon mustard
- 1 garlic clove, minced
- 2 tbsp fresh dill, finely chopped
- Salt and pepper, to taste

Instructions:

1.Prepare the Vegetables:
 In a large bowl, combine the thinly sliced cucumbers, red onion, and radishes. Toss gently to mix.

2.Make the Dressing:
 In a small bowl, whisk together the Greek yogurt, olive oil, lemon juice, Dijon mustard, garlic, dill, and a pinch of salt and pepper. Taste and adjust seasoning if needed.

3.Dress the Salad:
 Pour the Greek yogurt dill dressing over the cucumber mixture. Toss gently to ensure all the vegetables are evenly coated.

4.Chill and Serve:
 For the best flavor, cover the salad and chill in the refrigerator for at least 15 minutes before serving. Garnish with extra dill if desired.

Nutr. (Per Serving): Calories: 90 | Prot: 4g | Carbs: 6g | Fat: 5g | Fiber: 2g | Chol: 0mg | Na: 80mg | K: 200mg

Ingredients:

- 1 lb Brussels sprouts, trimmed and halved
- 2 tbsp extra virgin olive oil
- 1/4 tsp salt
- 1/4 tsp black pepper
- 2 tbsp balsamic vinegar
- 1 tsp honey (optional for added sweetness)

Instructions:

1.Preheat the Oven:
 Preheat your oven to 400°F (200°C).

2.Prepare the Brussels Sprouts:
 In a large bowl, toss the Brussels sprouts with olive oil, salt, and pepper until evenly coated.

3.Roast the Brussels Sprouts:
 Spread the Brussels sprouts in a single layer on a baking sheet lined with parchment paper. Roast in the preheated oven for 20-25 minutes, stirring halfway through, until they are golden brown and crispy.

4.Make the Balsamic Glaze:
 While the Brussels sprouts are roasting, heat the balsamic vinegar and honey (if using) in a small saucepan over medium heat. Simmer for about 5 minutes, or until the mixture has reduced and thickened into a glaze.

5.Finish the Dish:
 Once the Brussels sprouts are done, drizzle the balsamic glaze over them and toss gently to coat. Serve immediately.

Nutr. (Per Serving): Calories: 130 | Prot: 3g | Carbs: 11g | Fat: 9g | Fiber: 4g | Chol: 0mg | Na: 150mg | K: 350mg

Greek Salad with Kalamata Olives

Ingredients:

For the Salad:
- 2 cups cucumber, diced
- 1 cup cherry tomatoes, halved
- 1/2 red onion, thinly sliced
- 1/4 cup Kalamata olives, pitted and halved
- 1/4 cup feta cheese, crumbled (optional, can use reduced-fat feta)
- 1 tbsp fresh oregano, chopped

For the Vinaigrette:
- 2 tbsp extra virgin olive oil
- 1 tbsp lemon juice
- 1 tsp red wine vinegar
- 1 tsp Dijon mustard
- 1 garlic clove, minced
- Salt and pepper, to taste

Instructions:

1. Prepare the Vegetables:
   In a large salad bowl, combine the diced cucumber, cherry tomatoes, sliced red onion, and Kalamata olives.
2. Make the Vinaigrette:
   In a small bowl, whisk together the olive oil, lemon juice, red wine vinegar, Dijon mustard, garlic, salt, and pepper until well combined.
3. Dress the Salad:
   Drizzle the vinaigrette over the salad and toss gently to combine.

4. Optional Garnish:
   Sprinkle with feta cheese and fresh oregano for added flavor. Serve immediately.

Nutr. (Per Serving): Calories: 180 | Prot: 4g | Carbs: 7g | Fat: 14g | Fiber: 3g | Chol: 0mg (without feta) | Na: 300mg | K: 400mg

---

Lemon Herb Quinoa Pilaf

Ingredients:

- 1 cup quinoa, rinsed
- 2 cups low-sodium vegetable broth (or water)
- 1 tbsp extra virgin olive oil
- 1 tsp lemon zest
- 2 tbsp fresh lemon juice
- 2 tbsp fresh parsley, chopped
- 1 tbsp fresh cilantro, chopped (optional)
- 1 clove garlic, minced
- Salt and pepper, to taste

Instructions:

1. Cook the Quinoa:
   In a medium saucepan, bring the vegetable broth to a boil. Add the rinsed quinoa, reduce the heat to low, and cover. Simmer for about 15 minutes, or until the quinoa is cooked and the liquid is absorbed. Fluff with a fork.
2. Prepare the Dressing:
   In a small bowl, whisk together the olive oil, lemon zest, lemon juice, garlic, salt, and pepper.
3. Toss the Quinoa:
   Once the quinoa is cooked and fluffed, drizzle the lemon herb dressing over it and toss gently to combine.

4. Add the Herbs:
   Stir in the chopped parsley and cilantro (if using). Taste and adjust the seasoning with salt and pepper, if necessary.
5. Serve:
   Serve warm or at room temperature as a side dish or as a base for grilled vegetables or lean proteins.

Nutr. (Per Serving): Calories: 180 | Prot: 6g | Carbs: 27g | Fat: 6g | Fiber: 4g | Chol: 0mg | Na: 180mg | K: 220mg

Ingredients:

For the Salad:
- 1 cup canned kidney beans, rinsed and drained
- 1 cup canned chickpeas (garbanzo beans), rinsed and drained
- 1 cup fresh green beans, trimmed and blanched
- 1/4 red onion, thinly sliced
- 1/4 cup fresh parsley, chopped

For the Vinaigrette:
- 2 tbsp extra virgin olive oil
- 1 tbsp apple cider vinegar (or red wine vinegar)
- 1 tsp Dijon mustard
- 1 garlic clove, minced
- Salt and pepper, to taste

Instructions:

1. Prepare the Beans:
In a large salad bowl, combine the kidney beans, chickpeas, and blanched green beans. Add the sliced red onion and chopped parsley.

2. Make the Vinaigrette:
In a small bowl, whisk together the olive oil, vinegar, Dijon mustard, garlic, salt, and pepper.

3. Dress the Salad:
Pour the vinaigrette over the bean mixture and toss gently to combine.

4. Serve:
Serve the salad immediately or let it sit in the refrigerator for 15-20 minutes to allow the flavors to meld together.

Nutr. (Per Serving): Calories: 180 | Prot: 7g | Carbs: 22g | Fat: 8g | Fiber: 7g | Chol: 0mg | Na: 140mg | K: 400mg

Ingredients:

- 1 large head of cauliflower, cut into florets
- 3 garlic cloves, peeled
- 2 tbsp extra virgin olive oil
- 1/4 cup low-sodium vegetable broth (or water)
- Salt and pepper, to taste
- 1 tbsp fresh parsley or chives, chopped (optional garnish)

Instructions:

1. Cook the Cauliflower:
Bring a large pot of water to a boil. Add the cauliflower florets and garlic cloves. Cook for 10-12 minutes, or until the cauliflower is tender when pierced with a fork.

2. Drain and Mash:
Drain the cauliflower and garlic. Transfer them to a blender or food processor. Add the olive oil and vegetable broth, and blend until smooth and creamy. If you prefer a chunkier texture, use a hand masher instead.

3. Season:
Season the mashed cauliflower with salt and pepper to taste. Adjust the consistency with more vegetable broth if needed.

4. Serve:
Transfer the garlic mashed cauliflower to a serving bowl and garnish with fresh parsley or chives for added flavor and color.

Nutr. (Per Serving): Calories: 120 | Prot: 3g | Carbs: 10g | Fat: 7g | Fiber: 4g | Chol: 0mg | Na: 150mg | K: 320mg

Butternut Squash and Quinoa Side Dish

Ingredients:

- 1 cup quinoa, rinsed
- 2 cups low-sodium vegetable broth (or water)
- 2 cups butternut squash, peeled and diced into 1-inch cubes
- 1 tbsp extra virgin olive oil
- 1/2 tsp garlic powder
- 1/4 tsp ground cumin (optional for a warm, earthy flavor)
- Salt and pepper, to taste
- 2 tbsp fresh parsley, chopped
- 1 tbsp fresh lemon juice (optional)

Instructions:

1.Preheat the Oven:
 Preheat your oven to 400°F (200°C). Line a baking sheet with parchment paper.

2.Roast the Butternut Squash:
 Toss the diced butternut squash with olive oil, garlic powder, salt, and pepper (and cumin, if using). Spread evenly on the prepared baking sheet and roast for 20-25 minutes, or until golden and tender, tossing halfway through.

3.Cook the Quinoa:
 While the squash is roasting, bring the vegetable broth to a boil in a medium saucepan. Add the rinsed quinoa, reduce the heat, cover, and simmer for 15 minutes, or until the quinoa is tender and the broth is absorbed. Fluff the quinoa with a fork.

4.Assemble the Dish:
 Once the squash is done, gently combine it with the cooked quinoa in a large bowl. Add the chopped parsley and a drizzle of lemon juice for brightness (optional). Adjust the seasoning with more salt and pepper if needed.

5.Serve:
 Serve warm as a side dish or light meal. Garnish with extra parsley if desired.

Nutr. (Per Serving): Calories: 200 | Prot: 6g | Carbs: 35g | Fat: 5g | Fiber: 5g | Chol: 0mg | Na: 120mg | K: 500mg

Garlic Roasted Sweet Potato Wedges

Ingredients:

- 2 large sweet potatoes, washed and cut into wedges
- 2 tbsp extra virgin olive oil
- 3 garlic cloves, minced
- 1/2 tsp paprika (optional for a smoky flavor)
- Salt and pepper, to taste
- 1 tbsp fresh parsley, chopped (for garnish)

Instructions:

1.Preheat the Oven:
 Preheat your oven to 425°F (220°C). Line a baking sheet with parchment paper.

2.Season the Sweet Potatoes:
 In a large bowl, toss the sweet potato wedges with olive oil, minced garlic, paprika (if using), salt, and pepper until well-coated.

3.Roast the Sweet Potatoes:
 Spread the seasoned sweet potato wedges in a single layer on the prepared baking sheet. Roast in the oven for 25-30 minutes, flipping halfway through, until they are golden brown and crispy on the edges.

4. Serve:
 Once roasted, transfer the wedges to a serving dish and garnish with freshly chopped parsley. Serve immediately.

Nutr. (Per Serving): Calories: 180 | Prot: 2g | Carbs: 30g | Fat: 7g | Fiber: 4g | Chol: 0mg | Na: 150mg | K: 400mg

Ingredients:

- 1 cup quinoa, rinsed
- 2 cups low-sodium vegetable broth (or water)
- 2 cups broccoli florets, chopped
- 1/4 cup low-fat mozzarella cheese, shredded (optional)
- 1/4 cup whole wheat breadcrumbs (optional for topping)
- 2 tbsp extra virgin olive oil
- 1 garlic clove, minced
- 1/2 tsp paprika (optional)
- Salt and pepper, to taste
- 1 tbsp fresh parsley, chopped (for garnish)

Instructions:

1.Cook the Quinoa:
 In a medium saucepan, bring the vegetable broth to a boil. Add the rinsed quinoa, reduce the heat, cover, and simmer for 15 minutes, or until the quinoa is tender and the liquid is absorbed. Fluff with a fork.

2.Blanch the Broccoli:
 While the quinoa is cooking, bring a pot of water to a boil. Add the broccoli florets and cook for 2-3 minutes until bright green and slightly tender. Drain and set aside.

3.Prepare the Casserole Base:
 In a large mixing bowl, combine the cooked quinoa and broccoli. Stir in the olive oil, minced garlic, salt, pepper, and paprika (if using). Mix well.

4.Assemble the Casserole:
 Preheat your oven to 375°F (190°C). Transfer the quinoa and broccoli mixture to a greased casserole dish. Sprinkle the low-fat mozzarella cheese and whole wheat breadcrumbs over the top (optional).

5.Bake the Casserole:
 Bake in the preheated oven for 15-20 minutes, or until the top is golden and crispy. Remove from the oven and garnish with freshly chopped parsley before serving.

Nutr. (Per Serving): Calories: 220 | Prot: 8g | Carbs: 30g | Fat: 8g | Fiber: 6g | Chol: 0mg | Na: 180mg | K: 400mg

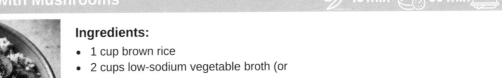
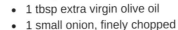

Ingredients:

- 1 cup brown rice
- 2 cups low-sodium vegetable broth (or water)
- 1 tbsp extra virgin olive oil
- 1 small onion, finely chopped
- 2 garlic cloves, minced
- 2 cups mushrooms, sliced (e.g., cremini or button)
- 1 tsp fresh thyme, chopped
- 2 tbsp fresh parsley, chopped
- Salt and pepper, to taste

Instructions:

1.Cook the Brown Rice:
 In a medium saucepan, bring the vegetable broth to a boil. Add the brown rice, reduce the heat, cover, and simmer for 30-35 minutes, or until the rice is tender and the liquid is absorbed. Fluff with a fork and set aside.

2.Sauté the Vegetables:
 In a large skillet, heat the olive oil over medium heat. Add the onion and garlic, and sauté for 3-4 minutes until softened. Add the mushrooms and cook for another 5-7 minutes, or until the mushrooms are tender and golden brown.

3.Combine the Rice and Vegetables:
 Add the cooked rice to the skillet with the mushrooms and stir to combine. Sprinkle in the fresh thyme, parsley, salt, and pepper. Stir well and cook for another 2-3 minutes to heat through.

4.Serve:
 Transfer the herbed brown rice with mushrooms to a serving dish and garnish with extra parsley if desired. Serve warm.

Nutr. (Per Serving): Calories: 210 | Prot: 6g | Carbs: 38g | Fat: 5g | Fiber: 4g | Chol: 0mg | Na: 120mg | K: 380mg

Chunky Vegetable and Barley Soup

⏱ 15 min | 🍲 30 min | 🛎 4 svgs.

Ingredients:

- 1 tbsp extra virgin olive oil
- 1 medium onion, chopped
- 2 garlic cloves, minced
- 2 carrots, peeled and chopped
- 2 celery stalks, chopped
- 1 medium zucchini, diced
- 3/4 cup tomatoes, chopped (or 1 can diced tomatoes, no salt added)
- 1/2 cup pearl barley, rinsed
- 5 cups low-sodium vegetable broth
- 1 tsp dried thyme
- 1/2 tsp dried oregano
- Salt and pepper, to taste

2 tbsp fresh parsley, chopped (for garnish)

Instructions:

1. Sauté the Vegetables:
Heat the olive oil over medium heat in a large pot. Add the onion, garlic, carrots, and celery, and sauté for 5-6 minutes until softened.

2. Add the Barley and Broth:
Stir in the rinsed barley and vegetable broth. Bring the mixture to a boil, then reduce the heat, cover, and simmer for about 25-30 minutes, or until the barley is tender.

3. Add the Remaining Vegetables:
Once the barley is cooked, add the zucchini, tomatoes, and herbs (thyme and oregano). Cook for an additional 10 minutes until the vegetables are tender.

4. Season and Serve:
Season with salt and pepper to taste. Garnish with fresh parsley and serve immediately.

Nutr. (Per Serving): Calories: 225 | Prot: 6g | Carbs: 30g | Fat: 4g | Fiber: 8g | Chol: 0mg | Na: 180mg | K: 450mg

Turkey and White Bean Chili

⏱ 10 min | 🍲 30 min | 🛎 4 svgs.

Ingredients:

- 1 tbsp olive oil
- 3/4 lb ground turkey (lean)
- 1 small onion, finely chopped
- 2 garlic cloves, minced
- 1 red bell pepper, diced
- 1 can (15 oz) white beans, drained and rinsed
- 1 can (14.5 oz) diced tomatoes (no salt added)
- 3/4 cup low-sodium chicken broth
- 1 1/2 tsp ground cumin
- 1/2 tsp chili powder
- 1/2 tsp paprika
- 1/4 tsp ground coriander
- Salt and pepper, to taste
- 1/4 cup fresh cilantro, chopped (optional garnish)
- Lime wedges, for serving (optional)

Instructions:

1. Cook the Ground Turkey:
In a large pot, heat the olive oil over medium heat. Add the ground turkey and cook for 6-8 minutes, breaking it into small pieces, until browned and fully cooked. Remove the turkey from the pot and set aside.

2. Sauté the Vegetables:
In the same pot, add the onion and garlic, cooking for 3-4 minutes until softened. Add the bell pepper and sauté for another 4-5 minutes until softened.

3. Add the Spices and Broth:
Stir in the cumin, chili powder, paprika, and ground coriander. Cook for 1-2 minutes until fragrant. Add the diced tomatoes, white beans, and chicken broth. Bring the mixture to a simmer.

4. Simmer the Chili:
Return the cooked turkey to the pot and stir everything together. Cover the pot and simmer for 15-20 minutes to allow the flavors to meld together.

5. Season and Serve:
Taste and adjust seasoning with salt and pepper as needed. Garnish with chopped cilantro and serve with lime wedges for added freshness.

Nutr. (Per Serving): Calories: 270 | Prot: 22g | Carbs: 22g | Fat: 8g | Fiber: 6g | Chol: 35mg | Na: 300mg | K: 510mg

Roasted Red Pepper and Tomato Soup

Ingredients:

- 4 large red bell peppers, halved and seeds removed
- 6 medium ripe tomatoes, quartered
- 1 medium onion, chopped
- 3 garlic cloves, minced
- 2 tbsp olive oil
- 3 cups low-sodium vegetable broth
- 1 tsp dried basil (or 1 tbsp fresh basil, chopped)
- 1/2 tsp dried thyme
- 1/2 tsp smoked paprika (optional, for extra flavor)
- Salt and pepper, to taste
- 1 tbsp balsamic vinegar (optional, for extra depth of flavor)
- Fresh basil or parsley, for garnish (optional)

Instructions:

1.Roast the Vegetables:
 Preheat your oven to 400°F (200°C). Place the red bell peppers and tomatoes on a baking sheet, drizzle with 1 tablespoon of olive oil, and season with salt and pepper. Roast for 25-30 minutes until the peppers are slightly charred and the tomatoes are soft.

2.Sauté the Onion and Garlic:
 While the vegetables are roasting, heat the remaining olive oil in a large pot over medium heat. Add the onion and cook for 5 minutes until softened. Add the garlic and cook for another minute until fragrant.

3.Blend the Vegetables:

Once the peppers and tomatoes are done roasting, add them to the pot with the onion and garlic. Pour in the vegetable broth, basil, thyme, and smoked paprika. Use an immersion blender or transfer to a blender in batches to blend until smooth.

4.Simmer the Soup:
 Bring the soup to a simmer over low heat and let it cook for 10-15 minutes to allow the flavors to meld. Stir in the balsamic vinegar (if using) for added depth.

5.Season and Serve:
 Taste and adjust the seasoning with salt and pepper as needed. Serve hot, garnished with fresh basil or parsley.

Nutr. (Per Serving): Calories: 170 | Prot: 3g | Carbs: 20g | Fat: 8g | Fiber: 6g | Chol: 0mg | Na: 300mg | K: 650mg

Spicy Lentil and Spinach Stew

Ingredients:

- 1 tbsp olive oil
- 1 small onion, chopped
- 2 garlic cloves, minced
- 1-inch piece of fresh ginger, grated
- 1 small green chili, finely chopped (optional, for extra spice)
- 1 tsp ground cumin
- 1 tsp ground coriander
- 1/2 tsp ground turmeric
- 1/2 tsp paprika
- 1/4 tsp cayenne pepper (optional, for extra heat)
- 1 cup dried red lentils, rinsed
- 4 cups low-sodium vegetable broth
- 2 cups fresh spinach, roughly chopped
- 1 can (14.5 oz) diced tomatoes, no salt added
- Salt and pepper, to taste
- 1 tbsp fresh lemon juice
- Fresh cilantro, for garnish (optional)

Instructions:

1.Sauté the Aromatics:
 Heat the olive oil in a large pot over medium heat. Add the onion, and sauté for 5 minutes until softened. Add the garlic, ginger, and green chili, and cook for 1-2 minutes until fragrant.

2.Add the Spices:
 Stir in the cumin, coriander, turmeric, paprika, and cayenne pepper. Cook the spices for about 1 minute, stirring constantly, to release their flavors.

3.Cook the Lentils:
 Add the lentils and stir to coat them in the spice mixture. Pour in the vegetable broth and diced tomatoes, and bring the mixture to a boil. Reduce the heat to low, cover, and let the stew simmer for

20-25 minutes until the lentils are tender and the stew has thickened.

4.Add the Spinach and Finish the Stew:
 Stir in the chopped spinach and cook for another 2-3 minutes until wilted. Add the lemon juice, and season with salt and pepper to taste.

5.Serve:
 Ladle the stew into bowls and garnish with fresh cilantro, if desired. Serve hot.

Nutr. (Per Serving): Calories: 210 | Prot: 12g | Carbs: 32g | Fat: 5g | Fiber: 9g | Chol: 0mg | Na: 120mg | K: 420mg

Sweet Potato and Kale Soup with Smoked Paprika

Ingredients:

- 1 tbsp olive oil
- 1 small onion, diced
- 2 garlic cloves, minced
- 1 tsp smoked paprika
- 1/2 tsp ground cumin
- 1/4 tsp red pepper flakes (optional, for extra heat)
- 2 large sweet potatoes, peeled and cubed
- 4 cups low-sodium vegetable broth
- 2 cups kale, stems removed, roughly chopped
- 1/2 tsp salt, or to taste
- 1/4 tsp black pepper
- 1 tbsp fresh lemon juice
- Fresh parsley, for garnish (optional)

Instructions:

1. Sauté the Aromatics:

In a large pot, heat the olive oil over medium heat. Add the onion and sauté for 5 minutes until softened. Add the garlic, smoked paprika, cumin, and red pepper flakes (if using), and cook for another minute until fragrant.

2. Cook the Sweet Potatoes:

Add the sweet potatoes to the pot, stirring to coat them in the spice mixture. Pour in the vegetable broth, bring to a boil, then reduce the heat to low. Cover and simmer for 15-20 minutes until the sweet potatoes are tender.

3. Add the Kale:

Stir in the chopped kale and cook for an additional 5 minutes until the kale is wilted and tender.

4. Season and Serve:

Stir in the lemon juice, and season the soup with salt and black pepper to taste. Ladle the soup into bowls and garnish with fresh parsley, if desired.

Nutr. (Per Serving): Calories: 220 | Prot: 5g | Carbs: 42g | Fat: 6g | Fiber: 8g | Chol: 0mg | Na: 300mg | K: 620mg

Sweet Mushroom and Wild Rice Stew

Ingredients:

- 1 tbsp olive oil
- 1 medium onion, chopped
- 2 garlic cloves, minced
- 1 1/2 cups cremini or button mushrooms, sliced
- 1/2 cup wild rice, rinsed
- 1 sweet potato, peeled and cubed
- 4 cups low-sodium vegetable broth
- 1/2 cup carrots, diced
- 1/2 cup celery, diced
- 1/2 tsp dried thyme
- 1/2 tsp dried rosemary
- 1 bay leaf
- Salt and pepper, to taste
- 2 tbsp fresh parsley, chopped (for garnish)
- 1 tbsp lemon juice (optional, for added brightness)

Instructions:

1. Sauté the Vegetables:

In a large pot, heat the olive oil over medium heat. Add the onion and sauté for 5 minutes until softened. Stir in the garlic and cook for another minute until fragrant.

2. Add the Mushrooms and Sweet Potato:

Add the mushrooms to the pot and cook for 4-5 minutes until they release their moisture and start to brown. Add the cubed sweet potato and cook for an additional 2 minutes, stirring frequently.

3. Cook the Wild Rice:

Add the wild rice, carrots, celery, vegetable broth, thyme, rosemary, and bay leaf. Bring the mixture to a boil, then reduce the heat to low, cover, and simmer for 40 minutes, or until the wild rice is tender and the vegetables are cooked through.

1. Season and Serve:

Remove the bay leaf and stir in the lemon juice (if using). Season with salt and pepper to taste. Ladle the stew into bowls and garnish with fresh parsley.

Nutr. (Per Serving): Calories: 250 | Prot: 6g | Carbs: 40g | Fat: 7g | Fiber: 6g | Chol: 0mg | Na: 180mg | K: 600mg

Italian Wedding Soup with Turkey Meatballs

Ingredients:

Ingredients: For the Meatballs:
- 1/2 lb ground turkey (lean)
- 1/4 cup whole wheat breadcrumbs
- 1 egg white
- 1 garlic clove, minced
- 2 tbsp fresh parsley, chopped
- 1/4 tsp black pepper
- 1/4 tsp salt (optional)

For the Soup:
- 1 tbsp olive oil
- 1 small onion, diced
- 1 large carrot, diced
- 1 celery stalk, diced
- 2 garlic cloves, minced
- 6 cups low-sodium chicken broth
- 1/4 cup uncooked whole wheat orzo (or other small whole grain pasta)
- 2 cups spinach or kale, chopped
- 1/2 tsp dried oregano
- Salt and pepper, to taste
- 1 tbsp fresh basil, chopped (optional)
- Freshly grated Parmesan cheese (optional)

Instructions:

1. Prepare the Meatballs:
   In a large bowl, combine the ground turkey, whole wheat breadcrumbs, egg white, minced garlic, parsley, salt (if using), and black pepper. Mix well and shape into small 1-inch meatballs. Set aside.

2. Sauté the Vegetables:
   In a large pot, heat the olive oil over medium heat. Add the diced onion, carrot, and celery, and sauté for 5 minutes until the vegetables are softened. Add the minced garlic and sauté for another minute.

3. Simmer the Soup:
   Pour in the low-sodium chicken broth and bring the mixture to a simmer. Once simmering, gently drop the turkey meatballs into the soup. Simmer for 15 minutes, or until the meatballs are cooked through.

4. Cook the Orzo and Greens:
   Stir in the whole wheat orzo and dried oregano. Simmer for another 8-10 minutes until the pasta is tender. Add the chopped spinach (or kale) in the last 2 minutes, allowing it to wilt into the soup.

5. Season and Serve:
   Season the soup with salt and pepper to taste. Ladle the soup into bowls and garnish with fresh basil and freshly grated Parmesan cheese if desired.

Nutr. (Per Serving): Calories: 280 | Prot: 23g | Carbs: 28g | Fat: 8g | Fiber: 4g | Chol: 45mg | Na: 180mg | K: 450mg

Vietnamese Pho with Rice Noodles and Tofu

Ingredients:

For the Broth:
- 8 cups low-sodium vegetable broth
- 1 large onion, halved
- 2-inch piece fresh ginger, sliced
- 1 cinnamon stick
- 4 star anise
- 4 whole cloves
- 1 tbsp soy sauce (low-sodium)
- 1 tbsp hoisin sauce
- 1 tbsp fish sauce (optional for flavor)

For the Pho:
- 8 oz rice noodles
- 1 block (14 oz) firm tofu, cubed
- 1 cup bean sprouts
- 1/2 cup fresh cilantro, chopped
- 1/2 cup fresh Thai basil leaves
- 1/4 cup green onions, chopped
- 1 lime, cut into wedges
- 1 small red chili, thinly sliced (optional)
- 1 tbsp olive oil
- Salt and pepper, to taste

Instructions:

1. Prepare the Broth:
   In a large pot, toast the cinnamon stick, star anise, cloves, onion, and ginger over medium heat for 2-3 minutes, until fragrant. Add the vegetable broth, soy sauce, hoisin sauce, and fish sauce (if using). Bring to a boil, then reduce heat and simmer for 20 minutes.

2. Cook the Tofu:
   In a skillet, heat the olive oil over medium heat. Add the tofu cubes and pan-fry until golden brown on all sides, about 8-10 minutes. Set aside.

3. Cook the Rice Noodles:
   Cook the rice noodles according to package instructions. Drain and set aside.

4. Strain the Broth:
   Remove the spices, onion, and ginger from the broth, leaving a clear and fragrant liquid. Season with salt and pepper to taste.

5. Assemble the Pho:
   Divide the cooked rice noodles into bowls. Top with tofu, bean sprouts, cilantro, Thai basil, and green onions. Pour the hot broth over the noodles and serve with lime wedges and chili slices (optional).

Nutr. (Per Serving): Calories: 320 | Prot: 13g | Carbs: 45g | Fat: 8g | Fiber: 4g | Chol: 0mg | Na: 480mg | K: 450mg

Seafood Cioppino with Shrimp and Cod

Ingredients:

- 1 tbsp olive oil
- 1 small onion, diced
- 4 garlic cloves, minced
- 1/2 cup celery, diced
- 1/2 cup fennel bulb, sliced thin
- 1/2 cup dry white wine (optional)
- 1 (14.5 oz) can diced tomatoes, no salt added
- 2 cups low-sodium vegetable or seafood broth
- 1 cup water
- 1 bay leaf
- 1/2 tsp dried oregano
- 1/2 tsp dried thyme
- 1/4 tsp red pepper flakes (optional)
- 1/2 lb shrimp, peeled and deveined
- 1/2 lb cod fillet, cut into 1-inch chunks
- 1/4 cup fresh parsley, chopped
- Salt and pepper, to taste
- 1 lemon, cut into wedges (for garnish)

Instructions:

1. Sauté the Vegetables:
   In a large pot, heat the olive oil over medium heat. Add the diced onion, garlic, celery, and fennel. Sauté for 5-7 minutes until softened and fragrant.

2. Deglaze with Wine (Optional):
   Pour in the white wine and allow it to simmer for 2-3 minutes, reducing slightly. If omitting wine, simply skip this step.

3. Add the Broth and Seasonings:
   Add the diced tomatoes, vegetable or seafood broth, water, bay leaf, oregano, thyme, and red pepper flakes (if using). Stir well and bring the mixture to a gentle simmer. Cook for 15 minutes to allow the flavors to meld

4. Add the Seafood:
   Gently add the shrimp and cod chunks to the simmering broth. Cook for an additional 5-7 minutes, until the seafood is opaque and fully cooked.

5. Season and Serve:
   Remove the bay leaf and season the cioppino with salt and pepper to taste. Ladle the soup into bowls, garnish with fresh parsley, and serve with lemon wedges on the side for a burst of brightness.

Nutr. (Per Serving): Calories: 240 | Prot: 26g | Carbs: 15g | Fat: 7g | Fiber: 3g | Chol: 90mg | Na: 300mg | K: 600mg

Creamy Cauliflower Soup

Ingredients:

- 1 large head of cauliflower, chopped
- 1 medium onion, diced
- 2 garlic cloves, minced
- 1 medium potato, peeled and diced
- 4 cups low-sodium vegetable broth
- 1 cup unsweetened almond milk (or any low-fat plant-based milk)
- 1 tbsp olive oil
- 1 tsp ground cumin
- 1/2 tsp smoked paprika (optional)
- Salt and pepper, to taste
- 1 tbsp fresh chives or parsley, chopped (for garnish)

Instructions:

1. Sauté the Vegetables:
   In a large pot, heat the olive oil over medium heat. Add the diced onion and sauté for 5 minutes until softened. Stir in the garlic and cook for another minute until fragrant.

2. Add the Cauliflower and Potato:
   Add the chopped cauliflower and diced potato to the pot. Sauté for 2-3 minutes, stirring frequently.

3. Simmer the Soup:
   Pour in the vegetable broth and bring to a boil. Lower the heat, cover, and simmer for 15-20 minutes, or until the cauliflower and potato are tender.

4. Blend the Soup:
   Remove the pot from heat and, using an immersion blender, blend the soup until smooth. Alternatively, transfer the soup in batches to a blender and blend until creamy.

5. Add Almond Milk and Season:
   Return the blended soup to the pot and stir in the almond milk. Season with cumin, smoked paprika (if using), salt, and pepper. Simmer for another 2-3 minutes, allowing the flavors to meld.

6. Serve:
   Ladle the soup into bowls and garnish with freshly chopped chives or parsley. Serve warm.

Nutr. (Per Serving): Calories: 170 | Prot: 5g | Carbs: 23g | Fat: 6g | Fiber: 5g | Chol: 0mg | Na: 150mg | K: 600mg

Smoky Black Bean and Sweet Potato Stew

Ingredients:

- 1 tbsp olive oil
- 1 small onion, diced
- 2 garlic cloves, minced
- 1 medium sweet potato, peeled and cubed
- 1 can (15 oz) black beans, drained and rinsed
- 1 can (14.5 oz) diced tomatoes, no salt added
- 2 cups low-sodium vegetable broth
- 1 tsp smoked paprika
- 1/2 tsp ground cumin
- 1/2 tsp chili powder
- 1/4 tsp cayenne pepper (optional, for heat)
- Salt and pepper, to taste
- 1/2 cup fresh cilantro, chopped (for garnish)
- 1 lime, cut into wedges (optional)

Instructions:

1. Sauté the Onion and Garlic:
In a large pot, heat the olive oil over medium heat. Add the diced onion and sauté for 4-5 minutes until softened. Add the minced garlic and cook for another minute until fragrant.

2. Add Sweet Potato and Spices:
Add the cubed sweet potatoes to the pot, along with the smoked paprika, cumin, chili powder, and cayenne pepper. Stir to coat the vegetables with the spices and cook for 2 minutes to let the flavors develop.

3. Simmer the Stew:
Add the diced tomatoes, black beans, and vegetable broth to the pot. Stir well to combine. Bring the mixture to a boil, then reduce the heat to low, cover, and let it simmer for 20-25 minutes, or until the sweet potatoes are tender and the stew has thickened.

4. Season and Garnish:
Taste and season with salt and pepper as needed. Once done, remove from heat and stir in half of the chopped cilantro. Serve the stew in bowls and garnish with the remaining cilantro and a squeeze of lime if desired.

Nutr. (Per Serving): Calories: 280 | Prot: 9g | Carbs: 50g | Fat: 6g | Fiber: 12g | Chol: 0mg | Na: 220mg | K: 750mg

Tuscan White Bean Soup with Rosemary

Ingredients:

- 1 tbsp olive oil
- 1 small onion, diced
- 2 garlic cloves, minced
- 2 medium carrots, diced
- 2 celery stalks, diced
- 1 tsp dried rosemary (or 2 fresh rosemary sprigs)
- 1 bay leaf
- 4 cups low-sodium vegetable broth
- 2 cans (15 oz) cannellini beans, drained and rinsed
- 1/2 cup whole grain farro or barley (optional for extra heartiness)
- Salt and pepper, to taste
- 1 tbsp lemon juice (optional, for brightness)
- Fresh parsley or rosemary, for garnish

Instructions:

1. Sauté the Vegetables:
In a large pot, heat the olive oil over medium heat. Add the diced onion, carrots, and celery, and sauté for 5-7 minutes until the vegetables are softened. Add the minced garlic and sauté for another minute until fragrant.

2. Add Broth and Beans:
Stir in the vegetable broth, white beans, rosemary, and bay leaf. If using farro or barley, add it now. Bring the mixture to a boil, then reduce heat and simmer for 25 minutes, stirring occasionally, until the grains (if using) are tender and the flavors meld together.

3. Season and Finish:
Remove the bay leaf and stir in the lemon juice (if using). Season the soup with salt and pepper to taste.

4. Serve and Garnish:
Ladle the soup into bowls and garnish with fresh parsley or rosemary. Serve with whole grain bread on the side for dipping.

Nutr. (Per Serving): Calories: 290 | Prot: 11g | Carbs: 45g | Fat: 7g | Fiber: 10g | Chol: 0mg | Na: 170mg | K: 510mg

Lentil and Carrot Stew with Coriander

Ingredients:

- 1 tbsp olive oil
- 1 small onion, finely chopped
- 2 garlic cloves, minced
- 1 1/2 cups red or green lentils, rinsed
- 4 medium carrots, peeled and diced
- 1 tsp ground coriander
- 1/2 tsp ground cumin
- 1/2 tsp turmeric (optional)
- 4 cups low-sodium vegetable broth
- 1 cup water (as needed)
- Salt and pepper, to taste
- 1 tbsp fresh coriander (cilantro), chopped (for garnish)
- 1 tbsp lemon juice (optional, for added brightness)

Instructions:

1.Sauté the Vegetables:
  In a large pot, heat the olive oil over medium heat. Add the chopped onion and sauté for 5 minutes until softened. Add the garlic and sauté for another minute, until fragrant.
2.Add the Spices and Lentils:
  Stir in the ground coriander, cumin, and turmeric (if using), and cook for 1 minute to toast the spices. Add the rinsed lentils and diced carrots, stirring to coat everything in the spice mixture.
3.Simmer the Stew:
  Pour in the vegetable broth and bring the mixture to a boil. Reduce the heat to low and let the stew simmer, covered, for 25-30 minutes, or until the lentils and carrots are tender. Stir occasionally, adding water if needed to reach your desired consistency.
4.Season and Finish:
  Once the stew is cooked, stir in the lemon juice (if using) and season with salt and pepper to taste.
5.Serve and Garnish:
  Ladle the stew into bowls and garnish with freshly chopped coriander (cilantro). Serve with whole-grain bread or a side salad for a complete, heart-healthy meal.

Nutr. (Per Serving): Calories: 230 | Prot: 12g | Carbs: 36g | Fat: 5g | Fiber: 12g | Chol: 0mg | Na: 160mg | K: 520mg

Classic Minestrone with Fresh Vegetables

Ingredients:

- 1 tbsp olive oil
- 1 small onion, diced
- 2 garlic cloves, minced
- 2 medium carrots, diced
- 2 celery stalks, diced
- 1 zucchini, diced
- 1 cup green beans, trimmed and cut into 1-inch pieces
- 1 can (14.5 oz) diced tomatoes, no salt added
- 4 cups low-sodium vegetable broth
- 1 can (15 oz) kidney beans, drained and rinsed
- 1/2 cup whole wheat elbow pasta (or small whole grain pasta of choice)
- 1/2 tsp dried oregano
- 1/2 tsp dried thyme
- 1/4 tsp black pepper
- Salt, to taste
- 1/4 cup fresh basil, chopped (for garnish)
- 1/4 cup grated Parmesan cheese (optional, for garnish)

Instructions:

1.Sauté the Vegetables:
  In a large pot, heat the olive oil over medium heat. Add the onion, carrots, and celery, and sauté for 5-6 minutes until softened. Add the garlic and cook for another minute until fragrant.
2.Add the Broth and Vegetables:
  Stir in the zucchini, green beans, diced tomatoes, and vegetable broth. Add the oregano, thyme, black pepper, and salt to taste. Bring the mixture to a boil, then reduce the heat to low and simmer for 15-20 minutes until the vegetables are tender.
3.Cook the Pasta and Beans:
  Stir in the kidney beans and whole wheat pasta. Simmer for an additional 10 minutes, or until the pasta is tender.
4.Garnish and Serve:
  Ladle the soup into bowls and garnish with fresh basil and a sprinkle of Parmesan cheese (if desired). Serve warm.

Nutr. (Per Serving): Calories: 250 | Prot: 9g | Carbs: 45g | Fat: 6g | Fiber: 10g | Chol: 0mg | Na: 180mg | K: 750mg

Vegetable Beef Stew with Lean Sirloin

Ingredients:

- 1 lb lean sirloin beef, cut into 1-inch cubes
- 1 tbsp olive oil
- 1 medium onion, diced
- 2 garlic cloves, minced
- 2 medium carrots, sliced
- 2 celery stalks, sliced
- 2 medium potatoes, diced
- 1 cup green beans, trimmed and cut into 1-inch pieces
- 1 can (14.5 oz) diced tomatoes, no salt added
- 4 cups low-sodium beef broth
- 1 tsp dried thyme
- 1 tsp dried rosemary
- 1 bay leaf
- Salt and pepper, to taste
- Fresh parsley, chopped (optional, for garnish)

Instructions:

1.Sear the Beef:
In a large pot or Dutch oven, heat the olive oil over medium heat. Add the sirloin cubes and sear for 3-4 minutes on each side until browned. Remove the beef from the pot and set aside.

2.Sauté the Vegetables:
In the same pot, add the diced onion, carrots, and celery. Sauté for 5-6 minutes until the vegetables are softened. Add the minced garlic and cook for another minute until fragrant.

3.Simmer the Stew:
Return the beef to the pot. Add the diced tomatoes, potatoes, green beans, beef broth, thyme, rosemary, and bay leaf. Stir well to combine. Bring the mixture to a boil, then reduce the heat to low, cover, and simmer for 1 hour or until the beef is tender and the vegetables are fully cooked.

4.Season and Serve:
Remove the bay leaf and season the stew with salt and pepper to taste. Garnish with fresh parsley if desired. Serve the stew hot in bowls for a hearty and nutritious meal.

Nutr. (Per Serving): Calories: 320 | Prot: 28g | Carbs: 30g | Fat: 10g | Fiber: 5g | Chol: 45mg | Na: 300mg | K: 900mg

Italian White Bean and Kale Stew

Ingredients:

- 1 tbsp extra virgin olive oil
- 1 small onion, diced
- 2 garlic cloves, minced
- 1 large carrot, diced
- 1 celery stalk, diced
- 1 (14.5 oz) can diced tomatoes, no salt added
- 1 (15 oz) can cannellini beans, drained and rinsed
- 4 cups low-sodium vegetable broth
- 3 cups fresh kale, chopped
- 1/2 tsp dried oregano
- 1/2 tsp dried thyme
- 1/4 tsp red pepper flakes (optional for heat)
- Salt and pepper, to taste
- 1 tbsp fresh parsley, chopped (for garnish)
- 1 tbsp lemon juice (optional, for added brightness)

Instructions:

1.Sauté the Vegetables:
In a large pot, heat the olive oil over medium heat. Add the diced onion, carrot, and celery. Sauté for 5-7 minutes until the vegetables are softened. Stir in the garlic and cook for another minute until fragrant.

2.Add the Broth and Beans:
Stir in the diced tomatoes, cannellini beans, vegetable broth, oregano, thyme, and red pepper flakes (if using). Bring the mixture to a simmer, then reduce the heat to low and let it cook for 15 minutes to allow the flavors to meld.

3.Add the Kale:
Add the chopped kale to the pot and stir well. Let the stew simmer for an additional 5-7 minutes, or until the kale is wilted and tender.

4.Season and Serve:
Stir in the lemon juice (if using) and season with salt and pepper to taste. Ladle the stew into bowls and garnish with freshly chopped parsley.

Nutr. (Per Serving): Calories: 220 | Prot: 10g | Carbs: 34g | Fat: 5g | Fiber: 10g | Chol: 0mg | Na: 240mg | K: 600mg

Baked Chicken Thighs with Garlic and Rosemary

⏱ 10 min · 🍳 35 min · 🔔 4 svgs.

Ingredients:

- 4 skinless, bone-in chicken thighs
- 2 tbsp olive oil
- 4 garlic cloves, minced
- 2 tbsp fresh rosemary, chopped (or 1 tsp dried rosemary)
- 1 tsp lemon zest (optional for brightness)
- Salt and pepper, to taste
- 1/2 tsp paprika (optional for color)
- 1/2 cup low-sodium chicken broth (or water)
- Fresh parsley, chopped (optional for garnish)

Customizable Ingredients:
- Vegetable options for roasting: Carrots, bell peppers, and sweet potatoes
- Whole grain options for serving: Brown rice, quinoa, or whole wheat couscous

Instructions:

1. Preheat the Oven:
 Preheat your oven to 400°F (200°C). Grease a baking dish with a little olive oil or use non-stick spray.

2. Prepare the Chicken:
 In a small bowl, mix the olive oil, minced garlic, rosemary, lemon zest (if using), salt, pepper, and paprika. Rub this mixture generously over the chicken thighs, making sure to coat each piece evenly.

3. Arrange the Chicken:
 Place the chicken thighs in the baking dish, bone-side down. Pour the low-sodium chicken broth around the chicken to keep it moist during baking.

4. Bake the Chicken:
 Bake for 30-35 minutes, until internal temperature reaches 165°F (74°C) and golden brown.

5. Roast the Vegetables (Optional):
 If adding vegetables, toss them with a little olive oil, salt, and pepper, and spread them on a separate baking sheet. Roast in the oven alongside the chicken for about 25-30 minutes, until tender and slightly caramelized.

6. Serve and Garnish:
 Once done, remove the chicken from the oven and let it rest for 5 minutes. Garnish with fresh parsley and serve with roasted vegetables and a side of whole grains.

Nutr. (Per Serving): Calories: 260 | Prot: 22g | Carbs: 4g | Fat: 18g | Fiber: 1g | Chol: 80mg | Na: 180mg | K: 450mg

Honey Mustard Glazed Turkey Tenderloin

⏱ 10 min · 🍳 25 min · 🔔 4 svgs.

Ingredients:

- 1 lb turkey tenderloin
- 2 tbsp honey
- 1 1/2 tbsp Dijon mustard
- 1 tbsp olive oil
- 1 garlic clove, minced
- 1 tbsp fresh lemon juice
- Salt and pepper, to taste
- 1/2 tsp paprika (optional for color)
- Fresh thyme or parsley, chopped (optional for garnish)

Customizable Ingredients:
- Vegetable options for roasting: Carrots, sweet potatoes, green beans, or Brussels sprouts
- Whole grain options for serving: Quinoa, brown rice, or farro

Instructions:

1. Preheat the Oven:
 Preheat your oven to 400°F (200°C) and line a baking sheet with parchment paper or lightly grease it with olive oil.

2. Prepare the Glaze:
 In a small bowl, mix honey, Dijon mustard, olive oil, garlic, lemon juice, salt, pepper, and paprika.

3. Season the Turkey:
 Place turkey tenderloin on the baking sheet and brush with half of the glaze.

4. Roast the Turkey:
 Roast for 20-25 minutes, until internal temperature reaches 165°F (74°C). Brush with remaining glaze halfway through.

5. Roast the Vegetables (Optional):
 If adding vegetables, toss them with a little olive oil, salt, and pepper, and spread them on a separate baking sheet. Roast alongside the turkey for 20-25 minutes until tender and slightly caramelized.

6. Rest and Slice:
 Once the turkey is fully cooked, remove it from the oven and let it rest for 5 minutes. Slice the tenderloin into medallions for serving.

7. Serve and Garnish:
 Serve with roasted vegetables and whole grains. Garnish with thyme or parsley.

Nutr. (Per Serving): Calories: 220 | Prot: 26g | Carbs: 10g | Fat: 8g | Fiber: 1g | Chol: 60mg | Na: 200mg | K: 450mg

Chicken and Quinoa Stuffed Bell Peppers

Ingredients:

- 4 large bell peppers (any color), tops cut off and seeds removed
- 1/2 cup quinoa, rinsed
- 1 cup low-sodium chicken broth (or water)
- 1/2 lb ground chicken breast (or diced cooked chicken breast)
- 1 small onion, diced
- 2 garlic cloves, minced
- 1 can (14.5 oz) diced tomatoes, no salt added

- 1 tsp dried oregano
- 1/2 tsp paprika (optional for color)
- Salt and pepper, to taste
- 1 tbsp olive oil
- Fresh parsley, chopped (for garnish)

Instructions:

1. Preheat the Oven:
 Preheat your oven to 375°F (190°C) and grease a baking dish large enough to hold the bell peppers upright.
2. Cook the Quinoa:
 In a saucepan, bring chicken broth (or water) to a boil. Add rinsed quinoa, cover, and simmer for 15 minutes until cooked. Fluff with a fork.
3. Sauté the Chicken and Vegetables:
 In a skillet, heat olive oil over medium heat. Cook onion for 3-4 minutes, then add garlic and ground chicken, cooking for 5-7 minutes until done (or add cooked chicken at this stage).
4. Add the Tomatoes and Seasonings:

 Stir in tomatoes, oregano, paprika, salt, and pepper. Simmer for 5 minutes, then mix in cooked quinoa.
5. Stuff the Bell Peppers:
 Fill each bell pepper with the chicken and quinoa mixture, pressing down slightly to pack the filling. Place the stuffed peppers upright in the greased baking dish.
6. Bake the Peppers:
 Bake in the preheated oven for 25-30 minutes, or until the peppers are tender and slightly golden on top.
7. Serve and Garnish:
 Let peppers cool slightly, garnish with parsley, and serve warm.

Nutr. (Per Serving): Calories: 290 | Prot: 24g | Carbs: 28g | Fat: 9g | Fiber: 6g | Chol: 40mg | Na: 220mg | K: 700mg

Spicy Cajun Grilled Chicken with Avocado Salsa

Ingredients:

For the Chicken:
- 4 skinless, boneless chicken breasts
- 1 tbsp olive oil
- 1 tbsp Cajun seasoning (store-bought or homemade)
- 1/2 tsp smoked paprika (optional for extra smokiness)
- 1/4 tsp cayenne pepper (optional for added heat)
- Salt and pepper, to taste

For the Avocado Salsa:
- 2 ripe avocados, diced
- 1 medium tomato, diced
- 1/4 cup red onion, finely diced
- 2 tbsp fresh cilantro, chopped
- Juice of 1 lime
- Salt and pepper, to taste

Instructions:

1. Preheat the Grill:
 Preheat your grill to medium-high heat (about 375°F / 190°C).
2. Season the Chicken:
 In a small bowl, mix together the Cajun seasoning, smoked paprika, cayenne pepper, salt, and pepper. Rub the olive oil and the spice mixture evenly over the chicken breasts.
3. Grill the Chicken:
 Place the chicken breasts on the preheated grill and cook for 6-8 minutes per side, or until the internal temperature reaches 165°F (74°C) and the chicken is fully cooked with nice grill marks.
4. Prepare the Avocado Salsa:

 While the chicken is grilling, combine the diced avocados, tomato, red onion, cilantro, and lime juice in a bowl. Season with salt and pepper to taste. Gently toss the ingredients to combine, being careful not to mash the avocado.
5. Serve the Chicken and Salsa:
 Once the chicken is done, let it rest for 5 minutes. Slice the chicken and serve it with a generous portion of avocado salsa on top or on the side.
6. Optional Grilled Vegetables:
 If grilling vegetables, toss them with a little olive oil, salt, and pepper, and grill them for 5-7 minutes alongside the chicken.

Nutr. (Per Serving): Calories: 320 | Prot: 30g | Carbs: 10g | Fat: 18g | Fiber: 7g | Chol: 75mg | Na: 220mg | K: 680mg

Cilantro Lime Chicken Tacos with Whole Wheat Tortillas

Ingredients:

For the Chicken:
- 1 lb skinless, boneless chicken breasts
- 2 tbsp olive oil
- 2 tbsp fresh lime juice
- 1 tbsp lime zest
- 2 tbsp fresh cilantro, chopped
- 2 garlic cloves, minced
- 1/2 tsp ground cumin
- 1/4 tsp chili powder
- Salt and pepper, to taste

For the Tacos:
- 8 small whole wheat tortillas
- 1 avocado, sliced
- 1 cup lettuce, shredded
- 1 medium tomato, diced
- 1/4 cup red onion, thinly sliced
- Fresh cilantro, chopped (for garnish)
- Lime wedges (for serving)

Instructions:

1. Marinate the Chicken:

 In a bowl, whisk together the olive oil, lime juice, lime zest, cilantro, minced garlic, cumin, chili powder, salt, and pepper. Add the chicken breasts to the marinade, coating them thoroughly. Let the chicken marinate for at least 15 minutes (or up to 2 hours in the refrigerator).

2. Grill the Chicken:

 Preheat a grill or grill pan over medium-high heat. Remove the chicken from the marinade and grill for 6-7 minutes per side, or until the chicken is cooked through and reaches an internal temperature of 165°F (74°C). Let the chicken rest for a few minutes before slicing it into thin strips.

3. Warm the Tortillas:

 While the chicken is resting, lightly warm the whole wheat tortillas on the grill or in a dry skillet for about 1 minute per side until soft and pliable.

4. Assemble the Tacos:

 Lay out the warm tortillas and top each one with the sliced chicken, avocado slices, lettuce, diced tomato, and red onion. Garnish with fresh cilantro and a squeeze of lime juice.

5. Serve:

 Serve the tacos with extra lime wedges on the side and your choice of salsa or low-fat Greek yogurt as a topping.

Nutr. (Per Serving): Calories: 320 | Prot: 25g | Carbs: 30g | Fat: 12g | Fiber: 8g | Chol: 55mg | Na: 180mg | K: 680mg

Oven-Roasted Lemon Pepper Turkey Cutlets

Ingredients:

- 1 lb turkey breast cutlets
- 2 tbsp olive oil
- 2 tbsp fresh lemon juice
- 1 tbsp lemon zest
- 1 tsp lemon pepper seasoning
- 1 garlic clove, minced
- Salt and pepper, to taste
- Fresh parsley, chopped (for garnish)
- Lemon slices (for garnish)

Customizable Ingredients:
- Vegetable options for roasting: Carrots, zucchini, bell peppers, or Brussels sprouts
- Whole grain options for serving: Quinoa, brown rice, or farro

Instructions:

1. Preheat the Oven:

 Preheat your oven to 400°F (200°C) and line a baking sheet with parchment paper or lightly grease it with olive oil.

2. Season the Turkey Cutlets:

 In a small bowl, whisk together the olive oil, lemon juice, lemon zest, minced garlic, lemon pepper seasoning, salt, and pepper. Rub the mixture over the turkey cutlets, ensuring they are evenly coated.

3. Arrange and Roast the Cutlets:

 Place the seasoned turkey cutlets on the prepared baking sheet in a single layer. Roast in the oven for 20-25 minutes, or until the cutlets reach an internal temperature of 165°F (74°C) and are golden brown.

4. Roast the Vegetables (Optional):

 If adding roasted vegetables, toss them with a little olive oil, salt, and pepper. Spread them on a separate baking sheet and roast alongside the turkey for 20-25 minutes until tender and slightly caramelized.

5. Garnish and Serve:

 Once the turkey cutlets are done, remove them from the oven and let them rest for a few minutes. Garnish with freshly chopped parsley and lemon slices before serving.

6. Serving Suggestions:

 Serve the turkey cutlets with roasted vegetables or your choice of whole grains for a balanced, heart-healthy meal.

Nutr. (Per Serving): Calories: 240 | Prot: 26g | Carbs: 4g | Fat: 12g | Fiber: 1g | Chol: 50mg | Na: 180mg | K: 450mg

Chicken and Spinach Skillet with Garlic

Ingredients:

- 1 lb skinless, boneless chicken breasts, cut into strips or bite-sized pieces
- 1 tbsp olive oil
- 3 garlic cloves, minced
- 6 cups fresh spinach, roughly chopped
- 1/4 cup low-sodium chicken broth (or water)
- 1/2 tsp ground black pepper
- 1/4 tsp salt (optional)
- 1 tbsp fresh lemon juice (optional)
- Fresh parsley, chopped (for garnish)

Customizable Ingredients:

- Vegetable options: Add mushrooms, bell peppers, or zucchini to the skillet for added nutrition.
- Whole grain options for serving: Quinoa, brown rice, or whole wheat couscous.

Instructions:

1. Heat the Oil:
 In a large skillet, heat the olive oil over medium heat. Once hot, add the chicken pieces in a single layer and cook for 4-5 minutes on each side until golden brown and cooked through. Remove the chicken from the skillet and set it aside.

2. Sauté the Garlic:
 In the same skillet, add the minced garlic and sauté for about 1 minute, until fragrant. Be careful not to let the garlic burn.

3. Add the Spinach and Broth:
 Add the fresh spinach to the skillet along with the low-sodium chicken broth. Stir occasionally until the spinach wilts, which should take about 2-3 minutes.

4. Combine and Season:
 Return the cooked chicken to the skillet and mix it with the spinach. Season with black pepper and salt (if using). Stir well to combine all the flavors. If desired, add a splash of fresh lemon juice for a burst of brightness.

5. Garnish and Serve:
 Once the chicken and spinach are heated through, remove from heat. Garnish with freshly chopped parsley and serve the dish alongside your choice of whole grains.

Nutr. (Per Serving): Calories: 220 | Prot: 30g | Carbs: 4g | Fat: 9g | Fiber: 2g | Chol: 65mg | Na: 170mg | K: 700mg

Greek-Style Chicken Souvlaki with Tzatziki

Ingredients:

For the Chicken Souvlaki:
- 1 lb skinless, boneless chicken breasts, cut into 1-inch cubes
- 2 tbsp olive oil
- 3 tbsp fresh lemon juice
- 1 tbsp lemon zest
- 3 garlic cloves, minced
- 2 tsp dried oregano
- 1/2 tsp ground black pepper
- Salt, to taste
- Fresh parsley, chopped (for garnish)

For the Tzatziki Sauce:
- 1 cup plain low-fat Greek yogurt
- 1/2 cucumber, finely grated (excess water squeezed out)
- 1 garlic clove, minced
- 1 tbsp fresh dill, chopped
- 1 tbsp fresh lemon juice
- Salt and pepper, to taste

Instructions:

1. Marinate the Chicken:
 In a bowl, mix the olive oil, lemon juice, lemon zest, minced garlic, oregano, black pepper, and salt. Add the cubed chicken, ensuring it is well-coated in the marinade. Cover and refrigerate for at least 30 minutes (or up to 2 hours for more flavor).

2. Prepare the Tzatziki Sauce:
 While the chicken is marinating, combine the Greek yogurt, grated cucumber, minced garlic, fresh dill, lemon juice, salt, and pepper in a bowl. Mix well, cover, and refrigerate until ready to serve.

3. Skewer and Grill the Chicken:
 Thread the marinated chicken cubes onto skewers. Preheat your grill or grill pan to medium-high heat. Grill the chicken for about 4-5 minutes on each side, or until the chicken is cooked through and has nice grill marks.

4. Serve:
 Remove the chicken from the skewers and serve it with the tzatziki sauce, whole wheat pita, and fresh vegetables. Garnish with fresh parsley and additional lemon wedges if desired.

Nutr. (Per Serving): Calories: 280 | Prot: 30g | Carbs: 8g | Fat: 14g | Fiber: 2g | Chol: 65mg | Na: 180mg | K: 500mg

Curry-Spiced Turkey Meatballs with Yogurt Sauce

⏱ 15 min 🍲 25 min 🍽 4 svgs.

Ingredients:

For the Meatballs:
- 1 lb ground turkey (lean)
- 1/4 cup whole wheat breadcrumbs
- 1 egg white
- 1 tbsp curry powder
- 1 garlic clove, minced
- 1 tsp ground cumin
- 1/2 tsp ground coriander
- 1/4 tsp black pepper
- 1/4 tsp salt (optional)
- 2 tbsp fresh cilantro, chopped

For the Yogurt Sauce:
- 1 cup plain low-fat Greek yogurt
- 1 tbsp fresh lemon juice
- 1/2 cucumber, grated and water squeezed out
- 1 garlic clove, minced
- 1 tbsp fresh mint or cilantro, chopped
- Salt and pepper, to taste

Instructions:

1. Preheat the Oven:
 Preheat your oven to 400°F (200°C) and line a baking sheet with parchment paper or lightly grease it.
2. Prepare the Meatballs:
 In a large bowl, mix together the ground turkey, whole wheat breadcrumbs, egg white, curry powder, minced garlic, cumin, coriander, black pepper, and salt (if using). Combine the mixture well and form into small 1-inch meatballs. Place the meatballs on the prepared baking sheet.
3. Bake the Meatballs:
 Bake the meatballs in the preheated oven for 20-25 minutes, or until they are cooked through and golden brown on the outside.

4. Prepare the Yogurt Sauce:
 While meatballs bake, mix Greek yogurt, lemon juice, grated cucumber, garlic, mint or cilantro, salt, and pepper in a bowl. Refrigerate until serving.
5. Serve the Meatballs:
 Once the meatballs are cooked, remove them from the oven and let them rest for a few minutes. Serve the meatballs with the yogurt sauce on the side and garnish with fresh cilantro if desired.
6. Serving Suggestions:
 Serve meatballs with whole grains (e.g., brown rice or quinoa) and steamed or roasted vegetables for a complete meal.

Nutr. (Per Serving): Calories: 250 | Prot: 30g | Carbs: 12g | Fat: 9g | Fiber: 2g | Chol: 50mg | Na: 220mg | K: 600mg

Baked Chicken Parmesan with Whole Wheat Breadcrumbs

⏱ 15 min 🍲 35 min 🍽 4 svgs.

Ingredients:

- 4 skinless, boneless chicken breasts (about 4 oz each)
- 1 cup whole wheat breadcrumbs
- 1/4 cup grated Parmesan cheese
- 1/2 tsp dried oregano
- 1/2 tsp garlic powder
- 1 egg white
- 1/4 cup low-fat milk or unsweetened almond milk
- 1 cup marinara sauce (low-sodium)
- 1/2 cup shredded part-skim mozzarella cheese
- Fresh basil, chopped (for garnish)
- Olive oil spray (for baking)

Customizable Ingredients:
- Vegetable options for serving: Roasted broccoli, zucchini, or bell peppers
- Whole grain options for serving: Whole wheat pasta, quinoa, or brown rice

Instructions:

1. Preheat the Oven:
 Preheat your oven to 400°F (200°C) and line a baking sheet with parchment paper. Lightly spray it with olive oil.
2. Prepare the Breading Station:
 In one shallow dish, whisk the egg white with the low-fat milk. In another shallow dish, combine the whole wheat breadcrumbs, grated Parmesan cheese, oregano, and garlic powder.
3. Bread the Chicken:
 Dip each chicken breast into the egg mixture, then coat it with the breadcrumb mixture, pressing gently to ensure the breadcrumbs adhere. Place the breaded chicken breasts on the prepared baking sheet.

4. Bake the Chicken:
 Lightly spray the tops of the chicken with olive oil spray. Bake the chicken in the preheated oven for 20 minutes. Then, remove from the oven and top each chicken breast with 2 tbsp of marinara sauce and 2 tbsp of shredded mozzarella.
5. Finish Baking:
 Return the chicken to the oven and bake for an additional 10 minutes, or until the chicken is cooked through and the cheese is melted and bubbly.
6. Garnish and Serve:
Remove chicken from oven, garnish with basil, and serve with whole grains and roasted vegetables.

Nutr. (Per Serving): Calories: 320 | Prot: 35g | Carbs: 18g | Fat: 10g | Fiber: 4g | Chol: 60mg | Na: 400mg | K: 500mg

BBQ Chicken Lettuce Wraps with Fresh Veggies

Ingredients:

For the Chicken:
- 1 lb skinless, boneless chicken breasts
- 1/2 cup low-sugar BBQ sauce (or homemade)
- 1 tbsp olive oil
- 1 tsp smoked paprika (optional for extra flavor)
- 1/4 tsp black pepper

For the Lettuce Wraps:
- 12 large lettuce leaves (butter lettuce or romaine)
- 1/2 cup shredded carrots
- 1/2 cucumber, julienned
- 1/2 red bell pepper, thinly sliced
- Fresh cilantro or parsley, chopped (for garnish)

Customizable Ingredients:
- Toppings: Add thinly sliced avocado or a sprinkle of sesame seeds for extra flavor.
- Sauce: Serve with a light yogurt-based dressing or extra BBQ sauce on the side.

Instructions:

1. **Cook the Chicken:**
Heat the olive oil in a large skillet over medium heat. Season the chicken breasts with black pepper and smoked paprika, then add them to the skillet. Cook for 5-6 minutes on each side, or until fully cooked. Once cooked, remove from the skillet and shred the chicken using two forks.

2. **Add the BBQ Sauce:**
Return the shredded chicken to the skillet and add the BBQ sauce. Stir well to coat the chicken in the sauce, and cook for another 2-3 minutes until the sauce is heated through.

3. **Prepare the Lettuce Wraps:**
While the chicken is cooking, wash and dry the lettuce leaves. Lay them out on a plate or serving platter.

4. **Assemble the Wraps:**
Spoon a portion of the BBQ chicken into each lettuce leaf. Top with shredded carrots, julienned cucumber, sliced red bell pepper, and garnish with fresh cilantro or parsley.

5. **Serve:**
Serve the wraps immediately with any additional toppings or sides you prefer.

Nutr. (Per Serving): Calories: 220 | Prot: 25g | Carbs: 12g | Fat: 8g | Fiber: 3g | Chol: 60mg | Na: 280mg | K: 600mg

Chicken Thighs with Lentils and Roasted Red Peppers

Ingredients:

For the Chicken:
- 4 skinless, bone-in chicken thighs
- 1 tbsp olive oil
- 1 tsp dried oregano
- 1 tsp smoked paprika
- 2 garlic cloves, minced
- Salt and pepper, to taste

For the Lentils:
- 1 cup dried green or brown lentils, rinsed
- 1 tbsp olive oil
- 1 small onion, diced
- 2 garlic cloves, minced
- 1 tsp ground cumin
- 1/2 tsp ground coriander
- 3 cups low-sodium vegetable or chicken broth
- Salt and pepper, to taste

For the Roasted Red Peppers:
- 2 large red bell peppers, cut into strips
- 1 tbsp olive oil
- Salt and pepper, to taste

Instructions:

1. **Preheat the Oven:**
Preheat your oven to 400°F (200°C). Line a baking sheet with parchment paper or lightly grease it.

2. **Season and Bake the Chicken:**
Rub the chicken thighs with olive oil, oregano, smoked paprika, garlic, salt, and pepper. Place the chicken on the baking sheet and bake for 25-30 minutes, or until the internal temperature reaches 165°F (74°C) and the chicken is golden and cooked through.

3. **Cook the Lentils:**
While chicken bakes, heat 1 tbsp olive oil in a saucepan over medium heat. Sauté onion and garlic for 3-4 minutes. Add acumin, coriander, lentils, and broth. Bring to a boil, reduce heat, cover, and simmer for 20-25 minutes until lentils are tender. Season with salt and pepper.

4. **Roast the Red Peppers:**
While the lentils are cooking, toss the red pepper strips in 1 tbsp of olive oil, salt, and pepper. Spread them on a separate baking sheet and roast in the oven for 15-20 minutes, or until the peppers are soft and slightly charred.

5. **Serve the Dish:**
Once the chicken, lentils, and peppers are ready, arrange them on a plate. Garnish with fresh parsley or cilantro and serve with a side of quinoa or couscous if desired.

Nutr. (Per Serving): Calories: 350 | Prot: 30g | Carbs: 25g | Fat: 15g | Fiber: 8g | Chol: 80mg | Na: 300mg | K: 600mg

Chicken Shawarma Bowls with Tabbouleh

⏱ 20 min 🍲 25 min 🛎 4 svgs.

Ingredients:

- 1 lb skinless, boneless chicken breasts, cut into strips
- 1 tbsp olive oil
- 2 tsp ground cumin
- 1 tsp ground paprika
- 1 tsp ground coriander
- 1/2 tsp ground turmeric
- 1/2 tsp ground cinnamon
- 1/4 tsp cayenne pepper (optional)
- 2 garlic cloves, minced
- 2 tbsp fresh lemon juice
- Salt and pepper, to taste
- 1/2 cup bulgur wheat
- 1 cup boiling water
- 1 cup fresh parsley, finely chopped
- 1/2 cup fresh mint, chopped (optional)
- 1 medium tomato, diced
- 1/2 cucumber, diced
- 1/4 cup green onions, chopped
- 2 tbsp olive oil
- 2 tbsp fresh lemon juice
- Salt and pepper, to taste

Instructions:

1. Marinate the Chicken:

  In a bowl, combine the olive oil, cumin, paprika, coriander, turmeric, cinnamon, cayenne pepper (if using), minced garlic, lemon juice, salt, and pepper. Add the chicken strips, making sure they are well coated in the marinade. Cover and let the chicken marinate for at least 15 minutes (or up to 2 hours in the refrigerator).

2. Prepare the Tabbouleh:

  While the chicken is marinating, place the bulgur wheat in a bowl and pour the boiling water over it. Cover the bowl and let it sit for about 15 minutes until the bulgur has absorbed the water and is tender. Fluff the bulgur with a fork and allow it to cool slightly.

3. Mix the Tabbouleh:

  Combine cooled bulgur with parsley, mint, tomato, cucumber, and green onions. Drizzle with olive oil, lemon juice, and season with salt and pepper. Toss until well mixed.

4. Cook the Chicken:

  Heat a grill pan or skillet over medium-high heat. Add the marinated chicken strips and cook for 4-5 minutes on each side, or until the chicken is cooked through and has nice grill marks.

5. Assemble the Bowls:

  Divide tabbouleh into four bowls, top with grilled chicken. Add optional toppings like hummus, yogurt sauce, or avocado for extra flavor.

Nutr. (Per Serving): Calories: 350 | Prot: 28g | Carbs: 30g | Fat: 14g | Fiber: 8g | Chol: 65mg | Na: 180mg | K: 550mg

Turkish Chicken Kebab with Minted Yogurt Sauce

⏱ 15 min 🍲 20 min 🛎 4 svgs.

Ingredients:

For the Chicken Kebab:
- 1 lb skinless, boneless chicken breasts, cut into 1-inch cubes
- 1 tbsp olive oil
- 1 tbsp fresh lemon juice
- 2 tsp ground cumin
- 1 tsp ground coriander
- 1 tsp paprika
- 1/2 tsp ground cinnamon
- 1/4 tsp cayenne pepper (optional for heat)
- 2 garlic cloves, minced
- Salt and pepper, to taste

For the Minted Yogurt Sauce:
- 1 cup plain low-fat Greek yogurt
- 2 tbsp fresh mint, finely chopped
- 1 tbsp fresh lemon juice
- 1 garlic clove, minced
- Salt and pepper, to taste

Instructions:

1. Marinate the Chicken:

  In a bowl, mix the olive oil, lemon juice, cumin, coriander, paprika, cinnamon, cayenne pepper (if using), minced garlic, salt, and pepper. Add the chicken cubes and coat them thoroughly with the marinade. Cover and let the chicken marinate for at least 30 minutes (or up to 2 hours in the refrigerator).

2. Prepare the Minted Yogurt Sauce:

  While the chicken is marinating, combine the Greek yogurt, chopped mint, lemon juice, minced garlic, salt, and pepper in a bowl. Stir well and refrigerate until ready to serve.

3. Skewer and Grill the Chicken:

Preheat a grill or grill pan over medium-high heat. Thread the marinated chicken cubes onto skewers. Grill the chicken for 4-5 minutes on each side, or until fully cooked and nicely charred.

4. Serve the Kebab:

  Remove the chicken from the grill and serve with the minted yogurt sauce on the side. Garnish with additional fresh mint or lemon wedges if desired.

5. Suggested Pairings:

  Serve the kebabs with fresh vegetables or a grain like brown rice, quinoa, or whole wheat pita for a complete, heart-healthy meal.

Nutr. (Per Serving): Calories: 300 | Prot: 30g | Carbs: 8g | Fat: 15g | Fiber: 3g | Chol: 60mg | Na: 180mg | K: 500mg

Grilled Chicken Fillet with Pineapple Salsa

15 min | 15 min | 4 svgs.

Ingredients:

For the Chicken:
- 4 skinless, boneless chicken breasts (about 4 oz each)
- 1 tbsp olive oil
- 1 tsp ground cumin
- 1/2 tsp smoked paprika
- 1 garlic clove, minced
- 1 tbsp fresh lime juice
- Salt and pepper, to taste

For the Pineapple Salsa:
- 1 cup fresh pineapple, diced
- 1/4 cup red onion, finely diced
- 1/4 cup fresh cilantro, chopped
- 1 tbsp fresh lime juice
- 1/2 jalapeño, seeded and finely chopped (optional for heat)
- Salt and pepper, to taste

Instructions:

1. Preheat the Grill:
 Preheat your grill or grill pan over medium-high heat.
2. Marinate the Chicken:
 In a small bowl, mix together the olive oil, ground cumin, smoked paprika, minced garlic, lime juice, salt, and pepper. Rub the marinade evenly over the chicken breasts and let them sit for 10-15 minutes.
3. Prepare the Pineapple Salsa:
 While the chicken is marinating, combine the diced pineapple, red onion, cilantro, lime juice, and jalapeño (if using) in a bowl. Season with salt and pepper to taste. Set aside.

4. Grill the Chicken:
 Place the chicken breasts on the preheated grill and cook for about 6-7 minutes on each side, or until the chicken reaches an internal temperature of 165°F (74°C) and has nice grill marks.
5. Serve the Chicken:
 Once the chicken is grilled, remove it from the heat and let it rest for a few minutes. Serve the grilled chicken fillets topped with the fresh pineapple salsa.
6. Serving Suggestions:
 Pair the dish with a serving of quinoa, brown rice, or roasted vegetables for a heart-healthy meal.

Nutr. (Per Serving): Calories: 240 | Prot: 28g | Carbs: 12g | Fat: 8g | Fiber: 2g | Chol: 65mg | Na: 180mg | K: 500mg

Herb-Marinated Grilled Turkey Burgers

15 min | 15 min | 4 svgs.

Ingredients:

For the Turkey Burgers:
- 1 lb ground turkey (lean)
- 2 tbsp fresh parsley, chopped
- 1 tbsp fresh thyme, chopped
- 1 garlic clove, minced
- 1 tbsp olive oil
- 1 tsp Dijon mustard
- 1/2 tsp ground black pepper
- 1/4 tsp salt (optional)

For the Toppings:
- 4 whole wheat burger buns
- 1 avocado, sliced
- 1 large tomato, sliced
- 4 lettuce leaves
- Optional: Sliced red onions, low-fat Greek yogurt, or hummus as a spread

Instructions:

1. Prepare the Turkey Patties:
 In a large bowl, combine the ground turkey, chopped parsley, thyme, minced garlic, olive oil, Dijon mustard, black pepper, and salt (if using). Mix the ingredients well and form the mixture into 4 equal-sized patties.
2. Preheat the Grill:
 Preheat your grill or grill pan to medium-high heat. Lightly oil the grill grates to prevent sticking.
3. Grill the Turkey Patties:
 Place the turkey patties on the preheated grill and cook for 5-6 minutes on each side, or until the internal temperature reaches 165°F (74°C) and the patties are golden and slightly charred.

4. Prepare the Buns and Toppings:
 While the patties are grilling, lightly toast the whole wheat buns on the grill for about 1 minute. Prepare the toppings, including slicing the avocado and tomato and washing the lettuce.
5. Assemble the Burgers:
 Place each turkey patty on a whole wheat bun and top with lettuce, tomato, avocado slices, and any additional toppings of your choice.
6. Serve the Burgers:
 Serve the burgers immediately with a side of quinoa, brown rice, or a fresh salad for a complete heart-healthy meal.

Nutr. (Per Serving): Calories: 320 | Prot: 28g | Carbs: 30g | Fat: 12g | Fiber: 6g | Chol: 60mg | Na: 180mg | K: 550mg

Moroccan-Spiced Chicken with Couscous and Almonds

Ingredients:

- 1 lb skinless, boneless chicken breasts
- 1 tbsp olive oil
- 2 tsp ground cumin
- 1 tsp ground coriander
- 1 tsp paprika
- 1/2 tsp ground cinnamon
- 1/4 tsp ground turmeric
- 2 garlic cloves, minced
- 1 tbsp fresh lemon juice
- Salt and pepper, to taste
- 1 cup whole wheat couscous
- 1 1/4 cups low-sodium vegetable or chicken broth
- 1/4 cup slivered almonds, toasted
- 1 tbsp olive oil
- 2 tbsp fresh parsley or cilantro, chopped
- Salt and pepper, to taste

For the Roasted Vegetables (Optional):

- 2 carrots, sliced
- 1 zucchini, sliced
- 1 tbsp olive oil
- Salt and pepper, to taste

Instructions:

1. Preheat the Oven:
   Preheat your oven to 400°F (200°C) if roasting vegetables alongside the chicken.
2. Marinate the Chicken:
   In a small bowl, combine the olive oil, cumin, coriander, paprika, cinnamon, turmeric, garlic, lemon juice, salt, and pepper. Rub this mixture all over the chicken breasts and let them marinate for at least 10-15 minutes (or up to 2 hours in the fridge).
3. Roast the Vegetables (Optional):
   Toss the sliced carrots and zucchini with olive oil, salt, and pepper. Spread them out on a baking sheet and roast in the oven for 20-25 minutes until tender and slightly caramelized.

4. Cook the Chicken:
   Heat a grill pan or skillet over medium heat. Grill the marinated chicken breasts for 6-7 minutes on each side, or until the chicken reaches an internal temperature of 165°F (74°C) and is golden
5. Prepare the Couscous:
   While chicken cooks, bring broth to a boil. Stir in couscous, cover, and remove from heat. Let sit for 5 minutes, then fluff with a fork. Mix in toasted almonds, olive oil, salt, and pepper.
6. Serve the Dish:
   Slice the grilled chicken and serve it over the couscous. Garnish with fresh parsley or cilantro and serve with the roasted vegetables on the side.

Nutr. (Per Serving): Calories: 380 | Prot: 30g | Carbs: 30g | Fat: 14g | Fiber: 6g | Chol: 65mg | Na: 220mg | K: 600mg

One-Pot Chicken and Farro with Mushrooms

Ingredients:

- 1 lb skinless, boneless chicken breasts, cut into bite-sized pieces
- 1 tbsp olive oil
- 1 small onion, diced
- 2 garlic cloves, minced
- 8 oz mushrooms, sliced (cremini or white mushrooms)
- 1 cup farro, rinsed
- 2 1/2 cups low-sodium chicken broth
- 1 tsp dried thyme
- 1/2 tsp ground black pepper
- 1/4 tsp salt (optional)
- Fresh parsley, chopped (for garnish)

Customizable Ingredients:

- Vegetable options: Add spinach or kale for extra greens.
- Garnishes: Top with a squeeze of fresh lemon juice for added brightness.

Instructions:

1. Sauté the Chicken:
   Heat the olive oil in a large pot or Dutch oven over medium heat. Add the chicken pieces, season with a pinch of salt and pepper, and sauté for 5-7 minutes until lightly browned. Remove the chicken from the pot and set aside.
2. Sauté the Vegetables:
   In the same pot, add the diced onion and sliced mushrooms. Cook for 5-6 minutes, until the mushrooms are browned and the onion is softened. Add the garlic and cook for another 1-2 minutes until fragrant.
3. Cook the Farro:
   Add the rinsed farro to the pot along with the chicken broth,

thyme, black pepper, and the sautéed chicken. Stir well, bring the mixture to a boil, then reduce the heat to low. Cover the pot and let it simmer for 25-30 minutes, or until the farro is tender and the liquid is mostly absorbed.
4. Garnish and Serve:
   Once the farro is cooked and the chicken is tender, remove from heat. Garnish with freshly chopped parsley and serve hot.
5. Serving Suggestions:
   Serve the dish with a side of steamed broccoli or roasted carrots for extra vegetables. You can also sprinkle some toasted almonds or seeds for added texture.

Nutr. (Per Serving): Calories: 330 | Prot: 28g | Carbs: 36g | Fat: 8g | Fiber: 7g | Chol: 50mg | Na: 220mg | K: 620mg

Stuffed Chicken Breasts with Spinach and Feta

15 min | 30 min | 4 svgs.

Ingredients:

- 4 skinless, boneless chicken breasts
- 2 cups fresh spinach, chopped
- 1/4 cup crumbled feta cheese (low-fat or reduced-sodium)
- 1 garlic clove, minced
- 1 tbsp olive oil
- 1 tsp dried oregano
- 1 tbsp fresh lemon juice
- Salt and pepper, to taste
- Fresh parsley, chopped (for garnish)

Customizable Ingredients:

- Vegetable options for serving: Roasted carrots, zucchini, or bell peppers
- Whole grain options: Serve with a side of brown rice, quinoa, or whole wheat couscous for extra fiber.

Instructions:

1. Preheat the Oven:
 Preheat your oven to 375°F (190°C) and lightly grease a baking dish with olive oil.

2. Prepare the Spinach and Feta Filling:
 Heat 1 tsp olive oil in a pan over medium heat. Sauté spinach and garlic for 2-3 minutes until wilted. Remove from heat, mix with crumbled feta, and season with salt and pepper.

3. Stuff the Chicken Breasts:
 Using a sharp knife, cut a slit into the side of each chicken breast to create a pocket. Be careful not to cut all the way through. Stuff each chicken breast with the spinach and feta mixture, securing the opening with toothpicks if needed.

4. Season the Chicken:
 Brush the chicken breasts with olive oil and drizzle them with lemon juice. Sprinkle dried oregano, salt, and pepper over the chicken.

5. Bake the Chicken:
 Place the stuffed chicken breasts in the greased baking dish. Bake in the preheated oven for 25-30 minutes, or until the chicken reaches an internal temperature of 165°F (74°C) and is golden brown on the outside.

6. Serve and Garnish:
 Remove toothpicks, garnish chicken with parsley, and serve with roasted vegetables or whole grains.

Nutr. (Per Serving): Calories: 290 | Prot: 30g | Carbs: 4g | Fat: 14g | Fiber: 2g | Chol: 70mg | Na: 280mg | K: 450mg

Asian BBQ Chicken Thighs with Sesame Broccoli

10 min | 25 min | 4 svgs.

Ingredients:

For the Chicken Thighs:

- 4 skinless, bone-in chicken thighs
- 2 tbsp low-sodium soy sauce
- 1 tbsp honey or maple syrup
- 1 tbsp hoisin sauce
- 1 tbsp rice vinegar
- 1 tsp sesame oil
- 2 garlic cloves, minced
- 1 tsp fresh ginger, grated
- 1 tsp chili flakes (optional for spice)
- Fresh cilantro, chopped (for garnish)

For the Sesame Broccoli:

- 2 cups fresh broccoli florets
- 1 tbsp sesame oil
- 1 tbsp low-sodium soy sauce
- 1 tsp toasted sesame seeds
- 1 garlic clove, minced
- Salt and pepper, to taste

Instructions:

1. Prepare the Marinade for the Chicken:
 In a small bowl, whisk together the soy sauce, honey, hoisin sauce, rice vinegar, sesame oil, garlic, ginger, and chili flakes. Place the chicken thighs in a shallow dish or resealable bag and pour the marinade over them. Let them marinate for at least 15 minutes (or up to 2 hours in the refrigerator).

2. Preheat the Oven or Grill:
 If using the oven, preheat it to 400°F (200°C). If grilling, preheat the grill to medium heat.

3. Cook the Chicken:
 Remove the chicken thighs from the marinade, shaking off excess sauce. Place them on a baking sheet lined with parchment paper or directly on the grill. Roast or grill for 20-25 minutes, turning halfway through, until the chicken is cooked through and has reached an internal temperature of 165°F (74°C).

4. Prepare the Sesame Broccoli:
 While chicken cooks, steam broccoli for 4-5 minutes. In a small pan, heat sesame oil and sauté garlic for 1-2 minutes. Toss broccoli in garlic oil and soy sauce, sprinkle with sesame seeds, and season with salt and pepper.

5. Serve the Dish:
 Remove cooked chicken from oven or grill, garnish with cilantro. Serve with sesame broccoli and brown rice or quinoa.

Nutr. (Per Serving): Calories: 320 | Prot: 25g | Carbs: 22g | Fat: 14g | Fiber: 4g | Chol: 70mg | Na: 220mg | K: 500mg

Grilled Salmon with Lemon and Dill

🕙 10 min 🍳 15 min 🔔 4 svgs.

Ingredients:

- 4 (6 oz) salmon fillets, skin removed
- 2 tbsp olive oil
- 2 tbsp fresh lemon juice
- 1 tbsp fresh dill, chopped
- 1 lemon, sliced (for garnish)
- Salt and pepper, to taste
- Fresh dill sprigs (for garnish)

Customizable Ingredients:

- Vegetable options for serving: Steamed asparagus, broccoli, or green beans
- Grain options for serving: Brown rice, quinoa, or whole wheat couscous

Instructions:

1. Preheat the Grill:
 Preheat your grill to medium-high heat, about 375°F (190°C). Lightly oil the grill grates to prevent the salmon from sticking.

2. Prepare the Salmon:
 Brush each salmon fillet with olive oil and drizzle with fresh lemon juice. Sprinkle the chopped dill over the fillets and season with salt and pepper to taste.

3. Grill the Salmon:
 Place the salmon fillets on the preheated grill. Grill for about 4-5 minutes per side, or until the salmon is cooked through and flakes easily with a fork. The internal temperature should reach 145°F (63°C).

4. Garnish and Serve:
 Once cooked, remove the salmon from the grill and garnish with fresh dill sprigs and lemon slices. Serve with your choice of steamed vegetables and whole grains for a balanced, nutritious meal.

Nutr. (Per Serving): Calories: 320 | Prot: 30g | Carbs: 2g | Fat: 20g | Fiber: 1g | Chol: 55mg | Na: 180mg | K: 600mg

Baked Cod with Garlic and Herbs

🕙 10 min 🍳 15 min 🔔 4 svgs.

Ingredients:

- 4 (6 oz) cod fillets
- 2 tbsp olive oil
- 3 garlic cloves, minced
- 2 tbsp fresh parsley, chopped
- 1 tbsp fresh lemon juice
- 1 tsp lemon zest
- Salt and pepper, to taste
- Lemon wedges, for garnish
- Fresh parsley or dill, for garnish (optional)

Customizable Ingredients:

- Vegetable options for serving: Steamed broccoli, carrots, or roasted asparagus.
- Grain options for serving: Quinoa, brown rice, or couscous.

Instructions:

1. Preheat the Oven:
 Preheat your oven to 400°F (200°C) and line a baking sheet with parchment paper or lightly grease it with olive oil.

2. Prepare the Cod:
 Place the cod fillets on the prepared baking sheet. In a small bowl, mix the olive oil, minced garlic, chopped parsley, lemon juice, lemon zest, salt, and pepper. Brush the mixture generously over the cod fillets.

3. Bake the Cod:
 Bake the cod fillets in the preheated oven for 12-15 minutes, or until the fish is opaque and flakes easily with a fork. The internal temperature should reach 145°F (63°C).

4. Serve the Dish:
 Remove the cod from the oven and garnish with additional parsley or dill and lemon wedges. Serve the cod with a side of steamed vegetables and your choice of whole grains for a complete, balanced meal.

Nutr. (Per Serving): Calories: 240 | Prot: 30g | Carbs: 2g | Fat: 12g | Fiber: 1g | Chol: 60mg | Na: 180mg | K: 500mg

Ingredients:

- 4 (6 oz) tilapia fillets
- 1 tbsp olive oil
- 1 cup cherry tomatoes, halved
- 1/2 cup Kalamata olives, pitted and halved
- 2 garlic cloves, minced
- 1 tbsp fresh lemon juice
- 1 tsp dried oregano
- 1/4 tsp ground black pepper
- Salt, to taste

- Fresh basil or parsley, chopped (for garnish)

Customizable Ingredients:

- Vegetable options for serving: Steamed asparagus, green beans, or roasted zucchini.
- Grain options for serving: Quinoa, brown rice, or whole wheat couscous.

Instructions:

1. Preheat the Oven:
 Preheat your oven to 400°F (200°C) and lightly grease a baking dish with olive oil.

2. Prepare the Tilapia:
 Place the tilapia fillets in the greased baking dish. In a small bowl, mix the olive oil, garlic, lemon juice, oregano, black pepper, and a pinch of salt. Drizzle this mixture evenly over the tilapia fillets.

3. Add the Vegetables:
 Scatter the halved cherry tomatoes and Kalamata olives around the tilapia fillets in the baking dish.

4. Bake the Tilapia:
 Bake in the preheated oven for 15-20 minutes, or until the tilapia is opaque and flakes easily with a fork. The internal temperature should reach 145°F (63°C).

5. Garnish and Serve:
 Remove the dish from the oven and garnish with freshly chopped basil or parsley. Serve the tilapia with your choice of whole grains or steamed vegetables for a complete, heart-healthy meal.

Nutr. (Per Serving): Calories: 260 | Prot: 30g | Carbs: 6g | Fat: 12g | Fiber: 2g | Chol: 55mg | Na: 250mg | K: 650mg

Ingredients:

- 1 lb large shrimp, peeled and deveined
- 2 tbsp olive oil
- 2 tbsp fresh lemon juice
- 2 garlic cloves, minced
- 1 tsp lemon zest
- 1 tbsp fresh parsley, chopped (plus more for garnish)
- 1/4 tsp ground black pepper
- Salt, to taste
- Wooden or metal skewers

Customizable Ingredients:

- Vegetable options for serving: Grilled zucchini, bell peppers, or cherry tomatoes.
- Grain options for serving: Brown rice, quinoa, or couscous.

Instructions:

1. Prepare the Marinade:
 In a small bowl, whisk together the olive oil, lemon juice, lemon zest, minced garlic, parsley, black pepper, and a pinch of salt. Add the shrimp to the bowl and toss to coat. Let the shrimp marinate for 10-15 minutes.

2. Preheat the Grill:
 Preheat your grill or grill pan to medium-high heat.

3. Thread the Shrimp onto Skewers:
 If using wooden skewers, soak them in water for 15 minutes to prevent burning. Thread the marinated shrimp onto the skewers.

4. Grill the Shrimp:
 Place the shrimp skewers on the preheated grill and cook for about 2-3 minutes on each side, or until the shrimp turn pink and opaque with light grill marks.

5. Serve the Dish:
 Once the shrimp are cooked, remove them from the grill and garnish with additional fresh parsley and lemon wedges. Serve with grilled vegetables or a side of whole grains for a complete meal.

Nutr. (Per Serving): Calories: 180 | Prot: 24g | Carbs: 2g | Fat: 8g | Fiber: 0g | Chol: 120mg | Na: 200mg | K: 300mg

Fish Tacos with Cabbage Slaw and Cilantro-Lime Sauce

 15 min | 10 min | 4 svgs.

Ingredients:

For the Fish Tacos:
- 1 lb white fish (tilapia, cod, or halibut)
- 1 tbsp olive oil
- 1 tsp ground cumin
- 1/2 tsp smoked paprika
- 1/4 tsp chili powder
- Salt and pepper, to taste
- 8 small whole wheat or corn tortillas
- Lime wedges, for garnish
- Fresh cilantro, for garnish

For the Cabbage Slaw:
- 2 cups green cabbage, shredded
- 1/2 cup red cabbage, shredded
- 1/4 cup carrots, shredded
- 1 tbsp olive oil
- 2 tbsp fresh lime juice
- Salt and pepper, to taste

For the Cilantro-Lime Sauce:
- 1/2 cup low-fat Greek yogurt
- 2 tbsp fresh lime juice
- 1/4 cup fresh cilantro, chopped
- 1 garlic clove, minced, salt and pepper

Instructions:

1. Prepare the Fish:

 In a small bowl, mix the olive oil, cumin, smoked paprika, chili powder, salt, and pepper. Rub this mixture over the fish fillets. Preheat a grill or skillet over medium-high heat. Grill the fish for 3-4 minutes on each side until it is opaque and cooked through. Break the fish into large chunks.

2. Make the Cabbage Slaw:

 In a bowl, combine the shredded green and red cabbage, carrots, olive oil, lime juice, salt, and pepper. Toss until the vegetables are well coated and set aside.

3. Prepare the Cilantro-Lime Sauce:

 In a separate bowl, whisk together the Greek yogurt, lime juice, chopped cilantro, garlic, salt, and pepper. Set aside for drizzling over the tacos.

4. Assemble the Tacos:

 Warm the tortillas on the grill or in a skillet for 1-2 minutes. Place chunks of the grilled fish in each tortilla, top with a spoonful of cabbage slaw, and drizzle with the cilantro-lime sauce. Garnish with fresh cilantro and serve with lime wedges on the side.

Nutr. (Per Serving): Calories: 280 | Prot: 25g | Carbs: 25g | Fat: 10g | Fiber: 6g | Chol: 45mg | Na: 180mg | K: 550mg

Coconut-Crusted Salmon with Mango Salsa

15 min | 15 min | 4 svgs.

Ingredients:

For the Salmon:
- 4 (6 oz) salmon fillets
- 1/2 cup unsweetened shredded coconut
- 1/4 cup whole wheat breadcrumbs
- 2 tbsp olive oil
- 1 tbsp fresh lime juice
- 1 egg white (optional for binding)
- Salt and pepper, to taste

For the Mango Salsa:
- 1 ripe mango, diced
- 1/4 cup red onion, finely diced
- 1/4 cup fresh cilantro, chopped
- 1 tbsp fresh lime juice
- 1/2 jalapeño, seeded and finely diced (optional for spice)
- Salt and pepper, to taste

Instructions:

1. Preheat the Oven:

 Preheat your oven to 375°F (190°C) and line a baking sheet with parchment paper or lightly grease it.

2. Prepare the Coconut Coating:

 In a shallow bowl, mix the shredded coconut, breadcrumbs, and a pinch of salt and pepper. In a separate bowl, whisk the egg white (optional) and lime juice.

3. Coat the Salmon:

 Dip each salmon fillet into the egg white and lime juice mixture, then press the fillets into the coconut mixture, coating them evenly.

4. Bake the Salmon:

 Place the coated salmon fillets on the prepared baking sheet. Drizzle the olive oil over the top of the fillets. Bake in the preheated oven for 12-15 minutes, or until the salmon is cooked through and the coconut is golden brown.

5. Prepare the Mango Salsa:

 While the salmon is baking, combine the diced mango, red onion, cilantro, lime juice, and jalapeño (if using) in a bowl. Season with salt and pepper to taste.

6. Serve the Dish:

 Remove salmon from oven, top with fresh mango salsa. Serve with whole grains or grilled vegetables.

Nutr. (Per Serving): Calories: 350 | Prot: 28g | Carbs: 18g | Fat: 20g | Fiber: 4g | Chol: 55mg | Na: 150mg | K: 600mg

Seafood Paella with Brown Rice and Peppers

Ingredients:

- 1 cup brown rice
- 2 1/2 cups low-sodium vegetable or seafood broth
- 1 tbsp olive oil
- 1 small onion, diced
- 1 red bell pepper, diced
- 2 garlic cloves, minced
- 1/2 tsp smoked paprika
- 1/4 tsp saffron threads (optional)
- 1/2 cup diced tomatoes (no salt added)
- 1/2 lb shrimp, peeled and deveined
- 1/2 lb mussels, cleaned and debearded
- 1/4 cup fresh parsley, chopped
- Lemon wedges, for garnish
- Salt and pepper, to taste

Customizable Ingredients:
- Vegetable options: Add peas or green beans for extra color and nutrients.
- Seafood options: Substitute calamari, clams, or scallops for variety.

Instructions:

1. Cook the Brown Rice:
In a medium pot, bring the vegetable or seafood broth to a boil. Add the brown rice, reduce the heat, cover, and simmer for about 30-35 minutes, or until the rice is tender and the liquid is absorbed. Set aside.

2. Sauté the Vegetables:
Heat olive oil in a large skillet over medium heat. Sauté onion and bell pepper for 5-6 minutes until softened. Add garlic, smoked paprika, and saffron (if using), cooking for 1-2 minutes until fragrant.

3. Add the Tomatoes and Brown Rice:
Stir the diced tomatoes into the skillet with the vegetables. Add the cooked brown rice and stir everything together, allowing the flavors to blend for 3-4 minutes.

4. Cook the Seafood:
Nestle the shrimp and mussels into the rice mixture. Cover the skillet and cook for 5-6 minutes, or until the shrimp turn pink and the mussels open. Discard any mussels that do not open.

5. Serve and Garnish:
Remove the paella from heat and sprinkle with freshly chopped parsley. Serve with lemon wedges on the side for a burst of brightness.

Nutr. (Per Serving): Calories: 350 | Prot: 26g | Carbs: 45g | Fat: 8g | Fiber: 6g | Chol: 95mg | Na: 220mg | K: 500mg

Shrimp Stir-Fry with Vegetables and Brown Rice

Ingredients:

- 1 lb shrimp, peeled and deveined
- 1 tbsp olive oil
- 1 red bell pepper, sliced
- 1 cup broccoli florets
- 1 large carrot, sliced
- 2 garlic cloves, minced
- 1 tsp fresh ginger, grated
- 2 cups cooked brown rice
- 1 tbsp fresh lime juice
- 1/4 cup green onions, chopped (for garnish)
- 1 tbsp sesame seeds (optional, for garnish)

Customizable Ingredients:
- Vegetable options: Add zucchini, snow peas, or mushrooms for extra variety.
- Grain options: Substitute quinoa or couscous for the brown rice if preferred.

Instructions:

1. Prepare the Shrimp and Vegetables:
Heat the olive oil in a large skillet or wok over medium heat. Add the shrimp and cook for 2-3 minutes until they turn pink and opaque. Remove the shrimp from the skillet and set aside.

2. Stir-Fry the Vegetables:
In the same skillet, add the bell pepper, broccoli, carrot, and garlic. Stir-fry for 5-6 minutes until the vegetables are tender-crisp.

3. Add the Sauce and Rice:
Stir in the low-sodium soy sauce, fresh ginger, and lime juice. Add the cooked brown rice and mix well, cooking for another 2-3 minutes to heat through.

4. Return the Shrimp:
Add the cooked shrimp back to the skillet and toss everything together. Stir-fry for another minute until well combined and heated through.

5. Serve and Garnish:
Serve the stir-fry hot, garnished with chopped green onions and sesame seeds (if using).

Nutr. (Per Serving): Calories: 320 | Prot: 28g | Carbs: 35g | Fat: 9g | Fiber: 6g | Chol: 120mg | Na: 220mg | K: 450mg

Poached Salmon with Cucumber Yogurt Sauce

Ingredients:

For the Poached Salmon:
- 4 (6 oz) salmon fillets, skin removed
- 4 cups water
- 1/2 cup white wine (optional)
- 1 lemon, sliced
- 2 garlic cloves, crushed
- 1 bay leaf
- Fresh dill sprigs, for garnish
- Salt and pepper, to taste

For the Cucumber Yogurt Sauce:
- 1/2 cup low-fat Greek yogurt
- 1/2 cucumber, grated and squeezed to remove excess water
- 1 tbsp fresh lemon juice
- 1 tbsp fresh dill, chopped
- 1 garlic clove, minced
- Salt and pepper, to taste

Instructions:

1. Poach the Salmon:

In a large saucepan, bring the water, white wine (if using), lemon slices, garlic cloves, bay leaf, and a pinch of salt to a gentle simmer. Carefully add the salmon fillets and poach them for 10-12 minutes, or until the salmon is cooked through and flakes easily with a fork. Remove the salmon from the poaching liquid and set aside.

2. Prepare the Cucumber Yogurt Sauce:

In a small bowl, mix the Greek yogurt, grated cucumber, lemon juice, chopped dill, minced garlic, and a pinch of salt and pepper. Stir until well combined.

3. Serve the Dish:

Place the poached salmon on a plate and spoon the cucumber yogurt sauce over the top. Garnish with fresh dill sprigs and lemon wedges. Serve with a side of steamed vegetables and your choice of whole grains for a complete meal.

Nutr. (Per Serving): Calories: 310 | Prot: 30g | Carbs: 6g | Fat: 18g | Fiber: 2g | Chol: 60mg | Na: 180mg | K: 600mg

Teriyaki Glazed Salmon with Broccoli

Ingredients:

For the Salmon:
- 4 (6 oz) salmon fillets
- 1 tbsp olive oil
- 1/4 cup low-sodium teriyaki sauce
- 1 tbsp honey (optional, for added sweetness)
- 1 tbsp low-sodium soy sauce
- 1 garlic clove, minced
- 1 tsp fresh ginger, grated
- 1 tsp sesame seeds (optional, for garnish)

- 2 green onions, sliced (for garnish)

For the Broccoli:
- 3 cups broccoli florets
- 1 tbsp olive oil (optional, for drizzling)
- Salt and pepper, to taste

Customizable Ingredients:
- Grain options for serving: Brown rice, quinoa, or whole wheat couscous.
- Additional vegetables: Add carrots or bell peppers for extra color and nutrients.

Instructions:

1. Prepare the Teriyaki Glaze:

In a small bowl, whisk together the teriyaki sauce, honey (if using), soy sauce, minced garlic, and grated ginger. Set aside.

2. Cook the Salmon:

Heat the olive oil in a large skillet over medium heat. Place the salmon fillets in the skillet, skin side down if the skin is still on. Cook for 3-4 minutes, then flip the salmon and cook for another 2-3 minutes, or until the salmon is cooked through. Pour the teriyaki glaze over the salmon and cook for an additional minute, allowing the sauce to thicken and coat the fish.

3. Steam the Broccoli:

While the salmon is cooking, steam the broccoli florets in a steamer basket over boiling water for about 4-5 minutes until bright green and tender. Optionally, drizzle with olive oil and season with salt and pepper.

4. Serve the Dish:

Place the teriyaki glazed salmon on a plate, garnish with sesame seeds and green onions, and serve alongside the steamed broccoli. Add a side of brown rice or quinoa for a complete meal.

Nutr. (Per Serving): Calories: 350 | Prot: 30g | Carbs: 12g | Fat: 20g | Fiber: 4g | Chol: 55mg | Na: 200mg | K: 650mg

Ginger Garlic Shrimp with Soba Noodles

Ingredients:

- 1 lb shrimp, peeled and deveined
- 1 tbsp olive oil
- 1 tbsp fresh ginger, grated
- 3 garlic cloves, minced
- 1 tbsp low-sodium soy sauce
- 1 tbsp rice vinegar
- 1 tbsp honey (optional for sweetness)
- 8 oz soba noodles (or whole wheat spaghetti)
- 2 green onions, sliced (for garnish)
- 1 tsp sesame seeds (for garnish)
- Red chili slices (optional, for garnish)

Customizable Ingredients:
- Vegetable options: Add bell peppers, broccoli, or snow peas for extra nutrients.
- Grain options: Substitute soba noodles with brown rice or quinoa if desired.

Instructions:

1. Cook the Soba Noodles:
 Cook the soba noodles according to package instructions. Drain and set aside.

2. Sear the Shrimp:
 In a large skillet, heat the olive oil over medium heat. Add the shrimp and cook for 2-3 minutes on each side until they turn pink and are lightly golden. Remove the shrimp from the skillet and set aside.

3. Prepare the Ginger Garlic Sauce:
 In the same skillet, add the grated ginger and minced garlic. Sauté for 1-2 minutes until fragrant. Stir in the soy sauce, rice vinegar, and honey (if using). Let the sauce simmer for 2-3 minutes.

4. Toss the Noodles and Shrimp:
 Add the cooked soba noodles and shrimp back to the skillet. Toss everything together in the ginger garlic sauce until well coated. Cook for an additional 1-2 minutes to heat through.

5. Serve and Garnish:
 Divide the shrimp and soba noodles among plates. Garnish with sliced green onions, sesame seeds, and red chili slices (if using). Serve immediately.

Nutr. (Per Serving): Calories: 350 | Prot: 28g | Carbs: 35g | Fat: 10g | Fiber: 4g | Chol: 110mg | Na: 200mg | K: 450mg

Spicy Cajun Shrimp and Brown Rice Pilaf

Ingredients:

For the Shrimp:
- 1 lb shrimp, peeled and deveined
- 1 tbsp olive oil
- 1 tbsp Cajun seasoning
- 1/4 tsp smoked paprika
- 1/4 tsp garlic powder
- Salt and pepper, to taste

For the Brown Rice Pilaf:
- 1 cup brown rice
- 2 1/2 cups low-sodium vegetable broth
- 1 tbsp olive oil
- 1 small onion, diced
- 1/2 red bell pepper, diced
- 1 celery stalk, diced
- 2 garlic cloves, minced
- 1/4 tsp dried thyme
- 1/4 tsp black pepper
- Fresh parsley, chopped (for garnish)

Instructions:

1. Prepare the Brown Rice Pilaf:
 In a medium saucepan, heat the olive oil over medium heat. Add the diced onion, bell pepper, and celery, and sauté for 5-6 minutes until softened. Add the garlic, thyme, and black pepper, and cook for another minute. Stir in the brown rice and vegetable broth. Bring to a boil, then reduce heat, cover, and simmer for about 20-25 minutes, or until the rice is tender and the liquid is absorbed.

2. Cook the Shrimp:
 While the rice is cooking, toss the shrimp in a bowl with Cajun seasoning, smoked paprika, garlic powder, salt, and pepper. Heat olive oil in a skillet over medium-high heat. Add the seasoned shrimp and cook for 2-3 minutes on each side until they turn pink and are lightly seared.

3. Assemble the Dish:
 Once the rice is cooked, fluff it with a fork and stir in fresh parsley. Serve the shrimp over the brown rice pilaf, garnishing with more parsley if desired.

Nutr. (Per Serving): Calories: 380 | Prot: 28g | Carbs: 45g | Fat: 12g | Fiber: 5g | Chol: 120mg | Na: 220mg | K: 500mg

Roasted Trout with Lemon and Almonds

Ingredients:

- 4 (6 oz) trout fillets
- 2 tbsp olive oil
- 2 tbsp fresh lemon juice
- 1/4 cup sliced almonds, toasted
- 1 lemon, thinly sliced (for garnish)
- Salt and pepper, to taste
- Fresh parsley, chopped (for garnish)

Customizable Ingredients:
- Vegetable options: Serve with steamed green beans, asparagus, or roasted zucchini.
- Grain options: Pair with brown rice, quinoa, or whole wheat couscous.

Instructions:

1. Preheat the Oven:
 Preheat your oven to 400°F (200°C) and line a baking sheet with parchment paper or lightly grease it with olive oil.
2. Season the Trout:
 Place the trout fillets on the prepared baking sheet. Drizzle with olive oil and fresh lemon juice, then season with salt and pepper.
3. Roast the Trout:
 Roast the trout in the preheated oven for 12-15 minutes, or until the fish is opaque and flakes easily with a fork.

4. Toast the Almonds:
 While the trout is roasting, toast the sliced almonds in a dry skillet over medium heat for 2-3 minutes, stirring frequently until they are golden brown.
5. Serve the Dish:
 Once the trout is done, transfer the fillets to a serving plate. Garnish with the toasted almonds, lemon slices, and freshly chopped parsley. Serve alongside steamed vegetables and your choice of whole grains.

Nutr. (Per Serving): Calories: 320 | Prot: 26g | Carbs: 5g | Fat: 20g | Fiber: 3g | Chol: 60mg | Na: 180mg | K: 550mg

Shrimp and Zucchini Noodles with Basil Pesto

Ingredients:

For the Shrimp and Zucchini Noodles:
- 1 lb shrimp, peeled and deveined
- 2 tbsp olive oil
- 4 medium zucchinis, spiralized into noodles
- 1 garlic clove, minced
- Salt and pepper, to taste

For the Basil Pesto:
- 1/2 cup fresh basil leaves
- 1/4 cup pine nuts or walnuts

- 1/4 cup grated Parmesan cheese (optional, low-fat version)
- 1 garlic clove, minced
- 1/4 cup olive oil
- 2 tbsp fresh lemon juice
- Salt and pepper, to taste

Instructions:

1. Prepare the Pesto:
 In a food processor, combine the basil leaves, pine nuts (or walnuts), Parmesan cheese (if using), garlic, lemon juice, salt, and pepper. Pulse until the mixture is finely chopped. Slowly add the olive oil while processing until smooth. Set aside.
2. Cook the Shrimp:
 Heat 1 tablespoon of olive oil in a large skillet over medium heat. Add the shrimp and season with salt and pepper. Cook for 2-3 minutes on each side until the shrimp are pink and cooked through. Remove from the skillet and set aside.
3. Sauté the Zucchini Noodles:
In the same skillet, add the remaining tablespoon of olive oil and

minced garlic. Sauté for 1 minute until fragrant. Add the spiralized zucchini noodles and cook for 2-3 minutes, tossing gently until the noodles are tender.
4. Combine and Serve:
 Toss the zucchini noodles with the basil pesto until well coated. Add the cooked shrimp and gently mix. Serve the dish garnished with fresh basil leaves.

Nutr. (Per Serving): Calories: 320 | Prot: 25g | Carbs: 10g | Fat: 22g | Fiber: 4g | Chol: 130mg | Na: 210mg | K: 500mg

Ingredients:

For the Cod Fish Cakes:
- 1 lb cod fillets, cooked and flaked
- 1/2 cup whole wheat breadcrumbs
- 1 egg white
- 1 small onion, finely chopped
- 1 garlic clove, minced
- 2 tbsp fresh parsley, chopped
- 1 tbsp Dijon mustard
- 1 tbsp fresh lemon juice
- Salt and pepper, to taste
- 1 tbsp olive oil (for frying)

For the Lemon-Dill Sauce:
- 1/2 cup low-fat Greek yogurt
- 1 tbsp fresh dill, chopped
- 1 tbsp fresh lemon juice
- 1 tsp lemon zest
- Salt and pepper, to taste

Customizable Ingredients:
- Vegetable options: Serve with steamed broccoli, roasted carrots, or a side salad.
- Grain options: Pair with quinoa or brown rice for added fiber.

Instructions:

1. Prepare the Fish Cake Mixture:

In a large bowl, combine the flaked cod, breadcrumbs, egg white, onion, garlic, parsley, Dijon mustard, lemon juice, salt, and pepper. Mix until well combined. Form the mixture into small patties.

2. Cook the Fish Cakes:

In a large skillet, heat the olive oil over medium heat. Cook the fish cakes for 3-4 minutes on each side, or until they are golden brown and crispy.

3. Make the Lemon-Dill Sauce:

In a small bowl, whisk together the Greek yogurt, dill, lemon juice, lemon zest, salt, and pepper. Adjust seasoning to taste.

4. Serve the Dish:

Serve the cod fish cakes warm, topped with a dollop of lemon-dill sauce. Garnish with fresh dill and lemon wedges, and pair with steamed vegetables or a whole grain for a complete meal.

Nutr. (Per Serving): Calories: 280 | Prot: 28g | Carbs: 15g | Fat: 10g | Fiber: 3g | Chol: 50mg | Na: 180mg | K: 500mg

Ingredients:

- 4 (6 oz) salmon fillets
- 1 lb asparagus, trimmed
- 1 cup cherry tomatoes, halved
- 2 tbsp olive oil
- 2 garlic cloves, minced
- 1 lemon, thinly sliced
- 1 tbsp fresh dill, chopped (or parsley)
- Salt and pepper, to taste
- Parchment paper

Customizable Ingredients:
- Vegetable options: Add zucchini or bell peppers for more variety.
- Grain options: Serve with quinoa, brown rice, or whole wheat couscous.

Instructions:

1. Preheat the Oven:

Preheat your oven to 400°F (200°C). Cut four large pieces of parchment paper, about 12x16 inches each.

2. Prepare the Salmon Packets:

Place one salmon fillet in the center of each piece of parchment paper. Arrange the asparagus and cherry tomatoes around the salmon. Drizzle with olive oil and sprinkle with minced garlic, fresh dill (or parsley), salt, and pepper. Top each fillet with 1-2 lemon slices.

3. Fold the Parchment Packets:

Fold the parchment paper over the salmon and vegetables, crimping the edges tightly to create a sealed packet. Place the packets on a baking sheet.

4. Bake the Salmon:

Bake the salmon packets in the preheated oven for 15-20 minutes, or until the salmon is cooked through and flakes easily with a fork.

5. Serve the Dish:

Carefully open the parchment packets and transfer the salmon, asparagus, and cherry tomatoes to plates. Serve with a side of quinoa or brown rice for a complete meal.

Nutr. (Per Serving): Calories: 320 | Prot: 30g | Carbs: 8g | Fat: 18g | Fiber: 4g | Chol: 55mg | Na: 200mg | K: 600mg

Grilled Haddock with Dill and Lemon

Ingredients:

- 4 (6 oz) haddock fillets
- 2 tbsp olive oil
- 2 tbsp fresh lemon juice
- 1 tbsp fresh dill, chopped
- 1 garlic clove, minced
- Salt and pepper, to taste
- Lemon wedges, for garnish
- Fresh dill sprigs, for garnish

Customizable Ingredients:
- Vegetable options: Serve with steamed broccoli, green beans, or asparagus.
- Grain options: Pair with quinoa, brown rice, or whole wheat couscous for added fiber.

Instructions:

1. Preheat the Grill:
 Preheat your grill to medium-high heat. Brush the grill grates lightly with olive oil to prevent sticking.

2. Prepare the Haddock Fillets:
 In a small bowl, whisk together the olive oil, lemon juice, minced garlic, and chopped dill. Season the haddock fillets with salt and pepper on both sides, then brush the fillets generously with the lemon-dill mixture.

3. Grill the Haddock:
 Place the haddock fillets on the preheated grill. Cook for 3-4 minutes on each side, or until the fish is opaque and flakes easily with a fork. Be careful not to overcook.

4. Serve the Dish:
 Transfer the grilled haddock to plates and garnish with fresh dill sprigs and lemon wedges. Serve with your choice of steamed vegetables and whole grains for a complete meal.

Nutr. (Per Serving): Calories: 270 | Prot: 30g | Carbs: 3g | Fat: 15g | Fiber: 1g | Chol: 70mg | Na: 180mg | K: 500mg

Herb-Crusted Tilapia with Lemon Dill Yogurt Sauce

Ingredients:

- For the Tilapia:
- 4 (6 oz) tilapia fillets
- 1/2 cup whole wheat breadcrumbs
- 2 tbsp fresh parsley, chopped
- 1 tbsp fresh dill, chopped
- 1 garlic clove, minced
- 1 tbsp olive oil
- Salt and pepper, to taste
- For the Lemon Dill Yogurt Sauce:
- 1/2 cup low-fat Greek yogurt
- 1 tbsp fresh lemon juice
- 1 tsp lemon zest
- 1 tbsp fresh dill, chopped
- Salt and pepper, to taste

Customizable Ingredients:
- Vegetable options: Serve with steamed broccoli, green beans, or roasted carrots.
- Grain options: Pair with quinoa, brown rice, or whole wheat couscous.

Instructions:

1. Preheat the Oven:
 Preheat your oven to 400°F (200°C) and line a baking sheet with parchment paper.

2. Prepare the Herb Crust:
 In a small bowl, combine the whole wheat breadcrumbs, parsley, dill, garlic, olive oil, salt, and pepper. Mix well.

3. Coat the Tilapia:
 Place the tilapia fillets on the prepared baking sheet. Press the herb mixture onto the top of each fillet to form a crust.

4. Bake the Tilapia:
 Bake the tilapia fillets in the preheated oven for 12-15 minutes, or until the fish is golden brown and flakes easily with a fork.

5. Prepare the Lemon Dill Yogurt Sauce:
 In a small bowl, whisk together the Greek yogurt, lemon juice, lemon zest, fresh dill, salt, and pepper. Set aside.

6. Serve the Dish:
 Once the tilapia is done, serve it with a dollop of the lemon dill yogurt sauce. Garnish with fresh dill and lemon wedges. Pair with steamed vegetables and whole grains for a complete meal.

Nutr. (Per Serving): Calories: 290 | Prot: 32g | Carbs: 10g | Fat: 12g | Fiber: 2g | Chol: 65mg | Na: 180mg | K: 550mg

Lentil and Vegetable Shepherd's Pie with Mashed Potatoes
⏱ 20 min 🍳 40 min 🍽 4 svgs.

Ingredients:

For the Filling:
- 1 cup dried lentils, rinsed and cooked (or 1 can, drained)
- 1 tbsp olive oil
- 1 onion, diced
- 2 garlic cloves, minced
- 2 medium carrots, diced
- 1 cup frozen peas
- 1 cup vegetable broth (low-sodium)
- 1 tbsp tomato paste
- 1 tsp dried thyme
- 1 tsp dried rosemary
- Salt and pepper, to taste

For the Mashed Sweet Potatoes:
- 2 large sweet potatoes, peeled and cubed
- 1 tbsp olive oil
- 1/4 cup unsweetened almond milk (or low-fat milk)
- Salt and pepper, to taste

Instructions:

1. Prepare the Sweet Potatoes:
 Boil the cubed sweet potatoes in a large pot of water until tender, about 12-15 minutes. Drain and mash with olive oil, almond milk, salt, and pepper until smooth.

2. Cook the Filling:
 While the sweet potatoes are cooking, heat olive oil in a large skillet over medium heat. Sauté the onion, garlic, and carrots for 5-7 minutes, until softened. Add the cooked lentils, tomato paste, vegetable broth, thyme, rosemary, salt, and pepper. Let the mixture simmer for 10 minutes until thickened. Stir in the peas.

3. Assemble the Shepherd's Pie:
 Preheat the oven to 375°F (190°C). Transfer the lentil and vegetable filling to a baking dish. Spread the mashed sweet potatoes evenly over the top.

4. Bake the Pie:
 Bake the shepherd's pie in the preheated oven for 20-25 minutes, or until the top is golden and the filling is bubbling.

5. Serve:
 Allow the pie to cool for a few minutes before serving. Pair it with a side salad for added freshness.

Nutr. (Per Serving): Calories: 350 | Prot: 14g | Carbs: 60g | Fat: 8g | Fiber: 12g | Chol: 0mg | Na: 240mg | K: 850mg

Spinach and Mushroom Stuffed Portobello Mushrooms
⏱ 15 min 🍳 20 min 🍽 4 svgs.

Ingredients:

For the Stuffed Mushrooms:
- 4 large portobello mushrooms, stems removed
- 2 tbsp olive oil
- 1 small onion, diced
- 2 garlic cloves, minced
- 2 cups fresh spinach, chopped
- 1 cup mushrooms, diced (any variety)
- 1/4 cup low-fat feta cheese (optional)
- Salt and pepper, to taste

For the Balsamic Glaze:
- 1/4 cup balsamic vinegar
- 1 tsp honey or maple syrup (optional)

Customizable Ingredients:
- Vegetable options: Add bell peppers or zucchini to the stuffing for extra texture.
- Protein options: Add cooked quinoa or lentils to the stuffing for added fiber and protein.

Instructions:

1. Preheat the Oven:
 Preheat your oven to 375°F (190°C). Lightly brush the portobello mushrooms with olive oil and season with salt and pepper. Place them on a baking sheet and roast for 10 minutes to soften.

2. Prepare the Filling:
 While the mushrooms are roasting, heat olive oil in a skillet over medium heat. Sauté the diced onion and garlic for 2-3 minutes until softened. Add the diced mushrooms and cook for another 4-5 minutes. Stir in the spinach and cook until wilted. Season with salt and pepper.

3. Stuff the Mushrooms:
 Remove the portobello mushrooms from the oven. Divide the spinach and mushroom mixture evenly among the mushrooms. If using, sprinkle with low-fat feta cheese.

4. Make the Balsamic Glaze:
 In a small saucepan, bring the balsamic vinegar and honey (if using) to a simmer over medium heat. Cook for 5-7 minutes until the mixture thickens into a glaze.

5. Finish the Dish:
 Drizzle the balsamic glaze over the stuffed mushrooms. Serve warm, garnished with fresh herbs if desired.

Nutr. (Per Serving): Calories: 200 | Prot: 6g | Carbs: 12g | Fat: 14g | Fiber: 4g | Chol: 0mg | Na: 180mg | K: 450mg

Roasted Cauliflower Steaks with Tahini and Pomegranate Seeds ⏱ 10 min 🍲 30 min 🛎 4 svgs.

Ingredients:

- 1 large cauliflower head, sliced into 4 "steaks"
- 2 tbsp olive oil
- 1/2 tsp ground cumin
- 1/2 tsp smoked paprika
- Salt and pepper, to taste

For the Tahini Sauce:
- 1/4 cup tahini
- 1 tbsp lemon juice
- 1 garlic clove, minced
- 2-3 tbsp water (to thin the sauce)
- Salt, to taste

For Garnish:
- 1/4 cup pomegranate seeds
- Fresh parsley or cilantro, chopped (optional)

Customizable Ingredients:
- Vegetable options: Add roasted chickpeas or steamed broccoli for extra fiber.
- Grain options: Serve with quinoa or brown rice for a more substantial meal.

Instructions:

1. Preheat the Oven:
 Preheat your oven to 400°F (200°C) and line a baking sheet with parchment paper.
2. Season the Cauliflower:
 Brush the cauliflower steaks with olive oil on both sides. Season with cumin, smoked paprika, salt, and pepper.
3. Roast the Cauliflower:
 Place the cauliflower steaks on the prepared baking sheet and roast for 25-30 minutes, flipping halfway through, until golden brown and tender.

4. Prepare the Tahini Sauce:
 In a small bowl, whisk together the tahini, lemon juice, minced garlic, and salt. Gradually add water, 1 tablespoon at a time, until the sauce reaches your desired consistency.
5. Serve the Dish:
 Drizzle the roasted cauliflower steaks with tahini sauce and garnish with pomegranate seeds. Add fresh parsley or cilantro for extra color. Pair with a side of quinoa or brown rice for a complete meal.

Nutr. (Per Serving): Calories: 240 | Prot: 6g | Carbs: 17g | Fat: 18g | Fiber: 6g | Chol: 0mg | Na: 150mg | K: 550mg

Butternut Squash and Zucchini Lasagna with Cashew Cream ⏱ 20 min 🍲 40 min 🛎 4 svgs.

Ingredients:

For the Lasagna:
- 2 medium zucchinis, thinly sliced lengthwise
- 1 small butternut squash, peeled and sliced thinly
- 2 tbsp olive oil
- Salt and pepper, to taste
- Fresh herbs like basil or parsley (for garnish)

For the Cashew Cream:
- 1 cup raw cashews (soaked in water for
- at least 4 hours)
- 1/2 cup water (for blending)
- 1 tbsp lemon juice
- 1 garlic clove
- 1/2 tsp salt
- 1/4 tsp black pepper
- 1 tbsp nutritional yeast (optional, for a cheesy flavor)

Instructions:

1. Preheat the Oven:
 Preheat your oven to 375°F (190°C).
2. Prepare the Cashew Cream:
 Drain the soaked cashews and blend them with water, lemon juice, garlic, salt, pepper, and nutritional yeast (if using) in a high-speed blender until smooth and creamy. Set aside.
3. Prepare the Vegetables:
 Brush the sliced zucchini and butternut squash with olive oil and season with salt and pepper. Grill or roast the vegetables for 5-7 minutes to soften them slightly.
4. Assemble the Lasagna:
 In a baking dish, layer the zucchini and butternut squash slices,

alternating with dollops of cashew cream between each layer. Continue layering until all ingredients are used, finishing with a final layer of cashew cream on top.
5. Bake the Lasagna:
 Cover the dish with foil and bake in the preheated oven for 25 minutes. Remove the foil and bake for an additional 10-15 minutes until the top is golden and bubbling.
6. Serve:
 Let the lasagna cool for a few minutes before serving. Garnish with fresh herbs and enjoy alongside a light green salad or whole grains.

Nutr. (Per Serving): Calories: 320 | Prot: 8g | Carbs: 40g | Fat: 16g | Fiber: 7g | Chol: 0mg | Na: 180mg | K: 900mg

Ingredients:

For the Zucchini Noodles:
- 4 medium zucchinis, spiralized into noodles
- 1 tbsp olive oil

For the Avocado Lemon Pesto:
- 1 large ripe avocado
- 1/2 cup fresh basil leaves
- 1/4 cup pine nuts (or walnuts)
- 2 tbsp lemon juice
- 1 garlic clove
- 1/4 cup extra virgin olive oil
- Salt and pepper, to taste

For Garnish:
- Fresh basil leaves
- Lemon zest
- Pine nuts

Instructions:

1. Prepare the Pesto:

 In a food processor, combine the avocado, basil, pine nuts, lemon juice, garlic, and olive oil. Blend until smooth and creamy. Season with salt and pepper to taste.

2. Cook the Zucchini Noodles:

 Heat olive oil in a large skillet over medium heat. Add the spiralized zucchini noodles and sauté for 2-3 minutes until just tender. Be careful not to overcook, as the noodles can become soggy.

3. Toss with Pesto:

 Remove the zucchini noodles from heat and toss them with the avocado lemon pesto until well coated.

4. Serve:

 Divide the noodles into bowls and garnish with fresh basil leaves, lemon zest, and a sprinkle of pine nuts for extra texture and flavor.

Nutr. (Per Serving): Calories: 220 | Prot: 5g | Carbs: 10g | Fat: 19g | Fiber: 7g | Chol: 0mg | Na: 120mg | K: 650mg

Ingredients:

For the Eggplant:
- 2 large eggplants, sliced into 1/2-inch rounds
- 1/4 cup olive oil
- Salt and pepper, to taste

For the Tomato Sauce:
- 1 (28 oz) can crushed tomatoes, no salt added
- 3 garlic cloves, minced
- 1 tbsp olive oil
- 1/2 tsp dried oregano
- 1/4 tsp red pepper flakes (optional)
- Salt and pepper, to taste

For Assembly:
- 1 cup shredded part-skim mozzarella cheese
- 1/4 cup grated Parmesan cheese
- Fresh basil leaves, for garnish

Instructions:

1. Preheat the Oven:

 Preheat your oven to 400°F (200°C). Line two baking sheets with parchment paper.

2. Prepare the Eggplant:

 Brush eggplant slices with olive oil, season with salt and pepper. Arrange in a single layer on baking sheets and roast for 25 minutes, flipping halfway, until golden and tender.

3. Make the Tomato Sauce:

 While eggplant roasts, heat 1 tbsp olive oil in a saucepan over medium heat. Sauté garlic for 1-2 minutes until fragrant. Stir in crushed tomatoes, red pepper flakes (optional), salt, and pepper. Simmer for 10-15 minutes.

4. Assemble the Dish:

 In a baking dish, spread a layer of tomato sauce. Add half the roasted eggplant, more sauce, and sprinkle with mozzarella and Parmesan. Repeat layers with remaining eggplant, sauce, and cheese.

5. Bake:

 Bake the assembled dish in the oven for 15-20 minutes, until the cheese is melted and bubbly, and the top is lightly golden.

6. Garnish and Serve:

 Remove from the oven and let cool for a few minutes. Garnish with fresh basil leaves and serve alongside a light green salad or whole wheat pasta.

Nutr. (Per Serving): Calories: 310 | Prot: 10g | Carbs: 28g | Fat: 16g | Fiber: 8g | Chol: 15mg | Na: 280mg | K: 720mg

Ingredients:

For the Tofu and Vegetables:
- 1 block firm tofu, pressed and cut into cubes
- 1 tbsp cornstarch (optional, for extra crispiness)
- 2 tbsp sesame oil (divided)
- 2 cups broccoli florets
- 1 large carrot, sliced thinly
- 2 cloves garlic, minced
- 1 tsp fresh ginger, grated

For the Sesame Soy Glaze:
- 1/4 cup low-sodium soy sauce
- 1 tbsp rice vinegar
- 1 tbsp maple syrup (or honey)
- 1 tsp toasted sesame oil
- 1 tsp cornstarch (optional, for thickening)
- 1 tbsp water

For Garnish:
- 1 tbsp toasted sesame seeds
- Sliced green onions

Instructions:

1. Prepare the Tofu:
 Press the tofu to remove excess moisture, then cut it into cubes. Toss the tofu cubes in cornstarch (if using) to help them crisp up during cooking.

2. Stir-Fry the Tofu:
 Heat 1 tablespoon of sesame oil in a large skillet over medium heat. Add the tofu cubes and stir-fry for 5-7 minutes, until golden and crispy on all sides. Remove from the skillet and set aside.

3. Stir-Fry the Vegetables:
 In the same skillet, add the remaining sesame oil. Sauté the minced garlic and grated ginger for 30 seconds until fragrant. Add the broccoli and carrots and stir-fry for 4-5 minutes until they are tender-crisp.

4. Make the Sesame Soy Glaze:
 In a small bowl, whisk together the soy sauce, rice vinegar, maple syrup, toasted sesame oil, cornstarch (if using), and water. Pour this mixture into the skillet with the vegetables and bring to a simmer, allowing the sauce to thicken.

5. Combine and Serve:
 Return the crispy tofu to the skillet and toss to coat everything in the sesame soy glaze. Cook for an additional 1-2 minutes. Serve the dish hot, garnished with toasted sesame seeds and sliced green onions.

Nutr. (Per Serving): Calories: 220 | Prot: 12g | Carbs: 18g | Fat: 12g | Fiber: 5g | Chol: 0mg | Na: 430mg | K: 500mg

Ingredients:

For the Filling:
- 1 can (15 oz) black beans, drained and rinsed
- 1 cup sweet corn kernels (fresh or frozen)
- 1 small red onion, diced
- 1 garlic clove, minced
- 1 tsp cumin powder
- 1/2 tsp smoked paprika
- Salt and pepper, to taste

For the Enchiladas:
- 8 small corn tortillas
- 2 cups salsa verde (store-bought or homemade)
- 1 tbsp olive oil (optional, for tortilla softening)

For Garnish:
- Fresh cilantro, chopped
- 1 avocado, sliced
- Lime zest (optional)

Instructions:

1. Preheat the Oven:
 Preheat your oven to 375°F (190°C). Lightly grease a baking dish.

2. Prepare the Filling:
 In a skillet over medium heat, sauté the diced red onion and minced garlic until softened (about 3-4 minutes). Add the black beans, corn, cumin, smoked paprika, salt, and pepper. Cook for an additional 2-3 minutes until heated through, then remove from heat.

3. Warm the Tortillas (Optional):
 Brush tortillas with olive oil and warm in a skillet for 10-20 seconds per side to prevent cracking.

4. Assemble the Enchiladas:
 Spoon the black bean and corn filling into the center of each tortilla. Roll up the tortillas and place them seam-side down in the baking dish. Pour the salsa verde evenly over the top of the enchiladas.

5. Bake:
 Cover the dish with foil and bake for 20 minutes. Then, remove the foil and bake for an additional 5 minutes until the enchiladas are bubbly and slightly golden.

6. Garnish and Serve:
 Remove from oven, garnish with cilantro, avocado, and lime zest. Serve with extra salsa verde if desired.

Nutr. (Per Serving): Calories: 300 | Prot: 10g | Carbs: 45g | Fat: 9g | Fiber: 10g | Chol: 0mg | Na: 400mg | K: 550mg

Spicy Chickpea Patties with Tzatziki and Cucumber Slices
15 min | 20 min | 4 svgs.

Ingredients:
For the Chickpea Patties:
- 1 can (15 oz) chickpeas, drained and rinsed
- 1 small onion, finely diced
- 2 garlic cloves, minced
- 1/4 cup fresh parsley, chopped
- 1/2 tsp ground cumin
- 1/2 tsp ground coriander
- 1/4 tsp cayenne pepper (optional)
- 1/4 cup whole wheat breadcrumbs
- Cucumber slices
- 1 tbsp olive oil (for cooking)
- Salt and pepper, to taste

For the Tzatziki:
- 1 cup plain Greek yogurt (low-fat or dairy-free alternative)
- 1 small cucumber, grated and squeezed to remove excess water
- 1 garlic clove, minced
- 1 tbsp fresh dill or mint, chopped
- 1 tbsp lemon juice
- Salt and pepper, to taste

Instructions:

1. Prepare the Chickpea Patties:
 In a large bowl, mash the chickpeas with a fork or potato masher until mostly smooth, leaving some texture. Stir in the diced onion, garlic, parsley, cumin, coriander, cayenne pepper (if using), breadcrumbs, salt, and pepper. Mix well to form a dough-like consistency.

2. Shape the Patties:
 Form the chickpea mixture into small patties, about 2-3 inches in diameter.

3. Cook the Patties:
 Heat the olive oil in a large skillet over medium heat. Cook the patties for 3-4 minutes on each side until golden brown and crispy. Remove from heat and set aside.

4. Make the Tzatziki:
 In a bowl, combine the Greek yogurt, grated cucumber, garlic, fresh dill or mint, lemon juice, salt, and pepper. Stir well and adjust seasoning to taste.

5. Serve:
 Arrange the chickpea patties on a plate with cucumber slices. Serve with a side of tzatziki for dipping. Garnish with extra parsley or herbs for a fresh touch.

Nutr. (Per Serving): Calories: 260 | Prot: 10g | Carbs: 35g | Fat: 9g | Fiber: 8g | Chol: 0mg | Na: 320mg | K: 500mg

Mushroom, Leek, and Spinach Quiche with Almond Flour Crust
15 min | 35 min | 4 svgs.

Ingredients:
For the Almond Flour Crust:
- 1 1/2 cups almond flour
- 1/4 tsp sea salt
- 1 tbsp olive oil
- 1 tbsp water

For the Filling:
- 1 tbsp olive oil
- 1 cup mushrooms, sliced
- 1 leek, white and light green parts, thinly sliced
- 2 cups fresh spinach, chopped
- 3 large eggs (or cholesterol-free egg substitute)
- 1/2 cup unsweetened almond milk (or low-fat milk)
- 1/4 tsp black pepper
- Salt, to taste
- 1/4 tsp nutmeg (optional)

Instructions:

1. Preheat the Oven:
 Preheat your oven to 350°F (175°C). Lightly grease a 9-inch pie dish.

2. Make the Almond Flour Crust:
 In a medium bowl, combine the almond flour, sea salt, olive oil, and water. Mix until a dough forms. Press the dough evenly into the bottom and up the sides of the pie dish. Bake the crust for 10 minutes until lightly golden.

3. Prepare the Filling:
 In a skillet over medium heat, warm the olive oil. Add the mushrooms and leeks, and sauté for 5-7 minutes until softened. Stir in the chopped spinach and cook for an additional 2 minutes until wilted. Remove from heat.

4. Assemble the Quiche:
 In a bowl, whisk together the eggs, almond milk, pepper, salt, and nutmeg (if using). Stir in the sautéed vegetables. Pour the mixture into the pre-baked almond flour crust.

5. Bake the Quiche:
 Place the quiche in the oven and bake for 25 minutes, or until the center is set and the top is lightly golden.

6. Serve:
 Let the quiche cool for a few minutes before slicing. Garnish with fresh herbs if desired.

Nutr. (Per Serving): Calories: 250 | Prot: 9g | Carbs: 10g | Fat: 20g | Fiber: 3g | Chol: 60mg | Na: 220mg | K: 350mg

Ingredients:

For the Polenta:
- 1 cup cornmeal (polenta)
- 4 cups water or low-sodium vegetable broth
- 1 tbsp olive oil
- Salt and pepper, to taste

For the Ratatouille Vegetables:
- 1 small eggplant, diced
- 1 zucchini, diced
- 1 red bell pepper, diced
- 1 yellow bell pepper, diced

- 1 small onion, diced
- 2 cloves garlic, minced
- 1 can (14.5 oz) diced tomatoes, no salt added
- 1 tbsp olive oil
- 1 tsp dried oregano
- 1 tsp dried thyme
- Fresh basil, for garnish

Instructions:

1. Prepare the Polenta:

Bring 4 cups of water or vegetable broth to a boil in a large pot. Slowly whisk in the cornmeal, stirring constantly to prevent lumps. Reduce the heat and simmer, stirring frequently, for 20-25 minutes, until the polenta is thick and creamy. Stir in olive oil, and season with salt and pepper. Spread the polenta onto a greased baking sheet, about 1/2 inch thick, and let it cool.

2. Bake the Polenta Rounds:

Preheat the oven to 400°F (200°C). Once the polenta has set, cut it into rounds using a cookie cutter or the rim of a glass. Place the rounds on a parchment-lined baking sheet and bake for 15-20 minutes, or until lightly golden.

3. Cook the Ratatouille Vegetables:

While the polenta is baking, heat 1 tablespoon of olive oil in a large skillet over medium heat. Add the diced onion and garlic, and sauté for 3-4 minutes. Add the diced eggplant, zucchini, and bell peppers, and cook for another 8-10 minutes, until softened. Stir in the diced tomatoes, oregano, and thyme. Simmer for 10 minutes until the vegetables are tender and the flavors are well combined. Season with salt and pepper to taste.

4. Serve:

Place the baked polenta rounds on plates and spoon the ratatouille vegetables on top. Garnish with fresh basil.

Nutr. (Per Serving): Calories: 290 | Prot: 6g | Carbs: 42g | Fat: 9g | Fiber: 7g | Chol: 0mg | Na: 180mg | K: 600mg

Ingredients:

For the Fritters:
- 2 medium zucchinis, grated
- 2 medium carrots, grated
- 1/4 cup whole wheat flour
- 1 egg (or flax egg for vegan option)
- 2 tbsp chopped fresh parsley
- 1 clove garlic, minced
- 1/2 tsp ground cumin
- Salt and pepper, to taste
- 2 tbsp olive oil (for frying)

For the Herbed Yogurt Sauce:
- 1/2 cup plain Greek yogurt (or dairy-free alternative)
- 1 tbsp fresh lemon juice
- 1 tbsp chopped fresh dill or parsley
- 1 small garlic clove, minced
- Salt and pepper, to taste
- Optional Garnishes:
- Fresh parsley or dill for garnish
- Lemon wedges

Instructions:

1. Prepare the Fritter Batter:

Grate the zucchini and carrots, and squeeze out any excess moisture using a clean kitchen towel. In a large bowl, combine the grated vegetables with whole wheat flour, egg, parsley, garlic, cumin, salt, and pepper. Mix until well combined.

2. Cook the Fritters:

Heat olive oil in a large skillet over medium heat. Scoop 2-3 tablespoons of the fritter mixture into the pan, flattening each fritter slightly with the back of a spoon. Fry for about 3-4 minutes per side, or until golden brown and crispy. Transfer the cooked fritters to a plate lined with paper towels to drain any excess oil.

3. Make the Herbed Yogurt Sauce:

In a small bowl, whisk together the Greek yogurt, lemon juice, fresh herbs, garlic, salt, and pepper until smooth. Adjust seasoning to taste.

4. Serve:

Serve the fritters warm with the herbed yogurt sauce on the side. Garnish with additional fresh parsley or dill and lemon wedges if desired.

Nutr. (Per Serving): Calories: 180 | Prot: 7g | Carbs: 14g | Fat: 11g | Fiber: 3g | Chol: 40mg | Na: 220mg | K: 400mg

Ingredients:

For the Filling:
- 1 tbsp olive oil
- 1 medium onion, diced
- 2 garlic cloves, minced
- 2 cups mushrooms, sliced
- 1 medium carrot, diced
- 1 cup frozen peas
- 1 cup cooked green or brown lentils
- 1 tbsp tomato paste
- 1 tsp dried thyme
- 1 tsp dried rosemary
- Salt and pepper, to taste
- 1 cup vegetable broth

For the Mashed Cauliflower Topping:
- 1 large head of cauliflower, chopped
- 2 tbsp olive oil (or vegan butter)
- 1 garlic clove, minced
- Salt and pepper, to taste
- Fresh parsley, chopped (for garnish)

Instructions:

1. Prepare the Filling:

Heat olive oil in a large skillet over medium heat. Add the diced onion and sauté for 3-4 minutes until softened. Add garlic, mushrooms, and carrots, cooking for another 5-7 minutes until the vegetables soften. Stir in the tomato paste, thyme, rosemary, and season with salt and pepper. Add the cooked lentils, peas, and vegetable broth, simmering for 10 minutes until the mixture thickens slightly.

2. Make the Mashed Cauliflower:

Steam or boil the cauliflower until tender, about 10-12 minutes. Drain well. In a large bowl, mash the cauliflower with olive oil and minced garlic until smooth. Season with salt and pepper to taste.

3. Assemble and Bake the Pie:

Preheat your oven to 375°F (190°C). Spread the vegetable and lentil filling in an even layer in a baking dish. Top with the mashed cauliflower, spreading it evenly over the filling. Bake for 20 minutes until the cauliflower is golden brown.

4. Serve:

Garnish with freshly chopped parsley before serving.

Nutr. (Per Serving): Calories: 250 | Prot: 10g | Carbs: 32g | Fat: 9g | Fiber: 9g | Chol: 0mg | Na: 320mg | K: 650mg

Ingredients:

- 1 zucchini, diced
- 1 red bell pepper, diced
- 1 yellow bell pepper, diced
- 1 small red onion, sliced
- 1 tbsp olive oil
- 1/2 tsp cumin
- 1/2 tsp smoked paprika
- Salt and pepper, to taste
- 4 small whole wheat tortillas
- Olive oil spray (for crisping)
- 2 ripe avocados, mashed
- 1 tbsp fresh lime juice
- 1/4 cup diced red onion
- 1 small tomato, diced
- 1 tbsp fresh cilantro, chopped
- 2 medium tomatoes, diced
- 1 small jalapeño, minced (optional)
- 1/4 cup red onion, diced
- 1 tbsp fresh cilantro, chopped
- 1 tbsp lime juice

Instructions:

1. Roast the Vegetables:

Preheat your oven to 400°F (200°C). Toss the diced zucchini, bell peppers, and red onion in olive oil, cumin, smoked paprika, salt, and pepper. Spread the vegetables in a single layer on a baking sheet and roast for 20-25 minutes, or until tender and lightly charred.

2. Crisp the Tostadas:

While the vegetables are roasting, lightly spray the tortillas with olive oil and bake them on a separate baking sheet for 5-7 minutes until crispy. Set aside.

3. Prepare the Guacamole:

In a bowl, mash the avocados and stir in lime juice, red onion, diced tomato, cilantro, salt, and pepper. Adjust seasoning to taste.

4. Prepare the Salsa:

In another bowl, mix the diced tomatoes, jalapeño (if using), red onion, cilantro, lime juice, salt, and pepper. Set aside.

5. Assemble the Tostadas:

Spread a layer of guacamole on each crisped tortilla, top with the roasted vegetables, and spoon salsa over the top.

6. Serve:

Garnish with extra cilantro and lime wedges. Serve immediately while the tostadas are still crisp.

Nutr. (Per Serving): Calories: 280 | Prot: 6g | Carbs: 32g | Fat: 17g | Fiber: 8g | Chol: 0mg | Na: 220mg | K: 700mg

Ingredients:

- 1 tbsp olive oil
- 1 small onion, finely diced
- 2 garlic cloves, minced
- 2 cups mushrooms, finely chopped
- 1 carrot, finely grated
- 1 celery stalk, finely diced
- 1 cup cooked lentils (green or brown)
- 1 can (14.5 oz) crushed tomatoes, no salt added
- 1 tbsp tomato paste
- 1 tsp dried oregano

- 1 tsp dried basil
- 1/4 tsp red pepper flakes (optional)
- Salt and pepper, to taste
- 1/2 cup low-sodium vegetable broth
- 1 tbsp balsamic vinegar (for added depth)
- 8 oz whole wheat spaghetti
- 1/4 cup fresh basil or parsley, chopped
- Freshly grated Parmesan cheese (optional, for garnish)

Instructions:

1. Prepare the Bolognese Sauce:
 Heat the olive oil in a large skillet over medium heat. Add the diced onion and sauté for 5-7 minutes until softened. Add the minced garlic and cook for an additional minute until fragrant.

2. Add the Vegetables:
 Stir in the finely chopped mushrooms, grated carrot, and diced celery. Cook for 8-10 minutes, or until the vegetables release their moisture and begin to brown.

3. Add the Lentils and Tomatoes:
 Add the cooked lentils, crushed tomatoes, tomato paste, dried oregano, dried basil, red pepper flakes (if using), salt, pepper, and vegetable broth. Stir well to combine.

4. Simmer:
 Lower the heat and let the sauce simmer for 15 minutes, allowing the flavors to meld. Stir in the balsamic vinegar during the last few minutes of cooking.

5. Cook the Spaghetti:
 While the sauce simmers, cook the whole wheat spaghetti according to the package instructions in salted water until al dente. Drain and set aside.

6. Serve:
 Divide spaghetti into bowls, top with Mushroom Lentil Bolognese. Garnish with basil or parsley, and grated Parmesan if desired.

Nutr. (Per Serving): Calories: 360 | Prot: 14g | Carbs: 62g | Fat: 7g | Fiber: 14g | Chol: 0mg | Na: 280mg | K: 850mg

Ingredients:

- 4 large bell peppers (red, yellow, or green), tops cut off and seeds removed
- 1 tbsp olive oil
- 1 small onion, finely diced
- 2 garlic cloves, minced
- 1 cup mushrooms, finely chopped
- 1 cup cooked lentils
- 1/2 cup cooked brown rice
- 1 tsp dried oregano
- 1 tsp dried thyme

- Salt and pepper, to taste
- 1/4 cup tomato sauce (no salt added)
- 1 tbsp balsamic vinegar
- 1/4 cup fresh parsley, chopped (for garnish)

Instructions:

1. Prepare the Bell Peppers:
 Preheat the oven to 375°F (190°C). Slice the tops off the bell peppers and remove the seeds. Place the peppers in a baking dish, standing upright.

2. Sauté the Vegetables:
 Heat olive oil in a large skillet over medium heat. Add the diced onion and sauté for 5 minutes until softened. Add the minced garlic and chopped mushrooms, and cook for another 5-7 minutes, until the mushrooms release their moisture and begin to brown.

3. Combine the Filling:
 Stir in the cooked lentils, brown rice, oregano, thyme, salt, and

pepper. Mix well, then add the tomato sauce and balsamic vinegar. Cook for another 2-3 minutes, allowing the flavors to meld.

4. Stuff the Peppers:
 Fill each bell pepper with the lentil and rice mixture, pressing down slightly to compact the filling. Place the filled peppers in the prepared baking dish.

5. Bake and Serve:
 Cover with foil and bake for 30 minutes. Uncover and bake for 10 more minutes until peppers are tender and browned. Garnish with parsley and serve hot.

Nutr. (Per Serving): Calories: 250 | Prot: 10g | Carbs: 42g | Fat: 5g | Fiber: 10g | Chol: 0mg | Na: 200mg | K: 750mg

Ingredients:

For the Casserole:
- 1 cup quinoa, rinsed
- 2 cups low-sodium vegetable broth
- 1 can (15 oz) black beans, drained and rinsed
- 1 can (14 oz) enchilada sauce (low-sodium)
- 1 cup corn kernels (fresh or frozen)
- 1 small red onion, diced
- 1 tsp cumin
- 1 tsp chili powder
- Salt and pepper, to taste
- 1/2 cup shredded low-fat cheese (optional)
- Fresh cilantro, chopped (for garnish)

For the Avocado Salsa:
- 1 ripe avocado, diced
- 1 small tomato, diced
- 1/4 red onion, finely diced
- Juice of 1 lime
- 2 tbsp fresh cilantro, chopped
- Salt and pepper, to taste

Instructions:

1. Cook the Quinoa:

In a medium saucepan, bring the vegetable broth to a boil. Add the quinoa, cover, and reduce the heat to low. Simmer for 15 minutes or until the quinoa is cooked and the liquid is absorbed. Fluff with a fork.

2. Prepare the Filling:

In a large mixing bowl, combine the cooked quinoa, black beans, corn, red onion, cumin, chili powder, and enchilada sauce. Mix until well combined. Season with salt and pepper.

3. Assemble the Casserole:

Preheat your oven to 375°F (190°C). Grease a baking dish and spread the quinoa mixture evenly in the dish. Sprinkle shredded cheese on top, if using.

4. Bake the Casserole:

Place the casserole in the oven and bake for 20-25 minutes, or until the top is bubbly and golden.

5. Prepare the Avocado Salsa:

While the casserole is baking, prepare the avocado salsa. In a small bowl, combine the diced avocado, tomato, red onion, lime juice, and cilantro. Season with salt and pepper to taste.

6. Serve:

Once the casserole is ready, remove it from the oven and let it cool slightly. Serve each portion with a generous spoonful of avocado salsa on top, and garnish with fresh cilantro.

Nutr. (Per Serving): Calories: 300 | Prot: 10g | Carbs: 45g | Fat: 10g | Fiber: 8g | Chol: 0mg | Na: 350mg | K: 600mg

Ingredients:

- 2 cups whole grain macaroni or pasta of choice
- 2 cups butternut squash, peeled and cubed
- 1/2 cup unsweetened almond milk (or any low-fat plant-based milk)
- 1/4 cup nutritional yeast
- 1 tbsp olive oil
- 1 tsp garlic powder
- 1 tsp onion powder
- 1/2 tsp Dijon mustard
- Salt and pepper, to taste
- Fresh parsley, chopped (optional, for garnish)
- 1/4 cup whole wheat breadcrumbs (optional, for topping)

Instructions:

1. Cook the Pasta:

In a large pot, bring water to a boil. Cook the whole grain pasta according to package instructions. Drain and set aside.

2. Steam the Butternut Squash:

While the pasta is cooking, steam the cubed butternut squash until tender, about 10-12 minutes. Alternatively, you can roast it in the oven at 400°F (200°C) for 25-30 minutes until soft.

3. Blend the Sauce:

In a blender or food processor, combine the cooked butternut squash, almond milk, nutritional yeast, olive oil, garlic powder, onion powder, and Dijon mustard. Blend until smooth and creamy. Taste and season with salt and pepper as needed.

4. Combine the Pasta and Sauce:

Pour the sauce over the cooked pasta and stir to coat evenly. If the sauce is too thick, you can add a splash of almond milk to adjust the consistency.

5. Optional Topping:

Preheat the oven to 375°F (190°C). Transfer the mac and cheese to an oven-safe dish, sprinkle with whole wheat breadcrumbs, and bake for 10-12 minutes until the breadcrumbs are golden and crispy.

6. Serve:

Garnish with freshly chopped parsley if desired. Serve warm.

Nutr. (Per Serving): Calories: 310 | Prot: 11g | Carbs: 58g | Fat: 7g | Fiber: 10g | Chol: 0mg | Na: 180mg | K: 560mg

Baked Blueberry Oatmeal Cups

⏱ 10 min 🍲 25 min 🛎 4 svgs.

Ingredients:

- 2 cups old-fashioned rolled oats
- 1 tsp baking powder
- 1/2 tsp ground cinnamon
- 1/4 tsp salt
- 1 cup unsweetened almond milk (or any plant-based milk)
- 2 large egg whites
- 1/4 cup unsweetened applesauce
- 2 tbsp pure maple syrup or honey
- 1 tsp vanilla extract
- 1 cup fresh or frozen blueberries

- 1/4 cup chopped walnuts or almonds (optional, for crunch)

Customizable Ingredients:
- Swap blueberries for raspberries or diced apples
- Add a sprinkle of flaxseeds or chia seeds for extra fiber
- Use a dairy-free chocolate chip or shredded coconut for variety

Instructions:

1. Preheat the Oven:
   Preheat your oven to 350°F (175°C). Line a 12-cup muffin tin with paper liners or lightly spray with nonstick cooking spray.
2. Prepare the Dry Ingredients:
   In a large mixing bowl, combine the rolled oats, baking powder, ground cinnamon, and salt. Stir to distribute the dry ingredients evenly.
3. Mix the Wet Ingredients:
   In another bowl, whisk together the almond milk, egg whites, unsweetened applesauce, maple syrup (or honey), and vanilla extract.
4. Combine the Mixtures:

Pour the wet ingredients into the bowl with the dry ingredients. Stir until well combined. Gently fold in the blueberries and chopped nuts (if using), ensuring the berries are evenly distributed.

5. Fill the Muffin Tin:
   Evenly divide the oatmeal mixture among the 12 muffin cups, filling each about three-quarters full. The mixture will be wet, but it will set as it bakes.
6. Bake and Serve: Bake for 20-25 minutes until golden and set (a toothpick should come out clean). Let cool in tin for 5-10 minutes, then transfer to a wire rack to cool completely. Serve warm or at room temperature.

Nutr. (Per Serving): Calories: 120 | Prot: 4g | Carbs: 20g | Fat: 3g | Fiber: 3g | Chol: 0mg | Na: 90mg | K: 130mg

Vegan Chocolate Mousse Tart with Almond Crust

⏱ 15 min 🍲 10 min 🛎 4 svgs.

Ingredients:

For the Almond Crust:
- 1 1/2 cups almond flour (or finely ground almonds)
- 3 tbsp coconut oil, melted
- 2 tbsp maple syrup
- 1/4 tsp salt

For the Chocolate Mousse Filling:
- 1 1/2 cups silken tofu (drained)
- 1/2 cup dark chocolate (70% cacao or higher), melted
- 2 tbsp unsweetened cocoa powder

- 2 tbsp maple syrup (or to taste)
- 1 tsp vanilla extract
- 1/8 tsp salt

Garnishes:
- Fresh raspberries or strawberries (optional)
- Mint leaves (optional)
- Cocoa powder for dusting (optional)

Customizable Ingredients:
- Swap almond flour for ground hazelnuts for a different crust flavor.
- Top with toasted almonds for added texture.

Instructions:

1. Prepare Almond Crust:
   Preheat oven to 350°F (175°C). In a bowl, mix almond flour, coconut oil, maple syrup, and salt until combined. Press mixture evenly into a tart pan and compact. Bake for 8-10 minutes until edges are golden, then let cool.
2. Make Chocolate Mousse Filling:
   In a food processor or blender, combine the silken tofu, melted dark chocolate, cocoa powder, maple syrup, vanilla extract, and salt. Blend until smooth and creamy, pausing to scrape down the sides as needed. Taste and adjust sweetness by adding more maple syrup, if desired.

3. Assemble the Tart:
   Once the almond crust has cooled, pour the chocolate mousse filling into the crust and spread it out evenly with a spatula. Smooth the top to create a glossy, even surface.
4. Chill the Tart:
   Place the tart in the refrigerator and chill for at least 2 hours (or overnight) to allow the mousse to set and the flavors to develop.
5. Garnish and Serve:
   Before serving, garnish the tart with fresh raspberries, mint leaves, and a dusting of cocoa powder if desired. Slice and serve chilled.

Nutr. (Per Serving): Calories: 220 | Prot: 6g | Carbs: 18g | Fat: 15g | Fiber: 5g | Chol: 0mg | Na: 90mg | K: 250mg

Pumpkin Loaf with Maple Glaze

Ingredients:

For the Pumpkin Loaf:
- 1 1/2 cups whole wheat flour
- 1 tsp baking soda
- 1/2 tsp baking powder
- 1/2 tsp ground cinnamon
- 1/4 tsp ground nutmeg
- 1/4 tsp ground ginger
- 1/4 tsp salt
- 1 cup pure pumpkin puree
- 1/4 cup unsweetened applesauce
- 1/4 cup pure maple syrup
- 2 large egg whites
- 1 tsp vanilla extract
- 1/4 cup unsweetened almond milk

For the Maple Glaze:
- 2 tbsp pure maple syrup
- 1/4 cup powdered sugar (optional, or substitute with a healthier alternative like monk fruit powder)
- 1 tsp almond milk

Instructions:

1. **Preheat Oven:**
   Preheat oven to 350°F (175°C). Grease a 9x5-inch loaf pan or line with parchment paper.
2. **Dry Ingredients:**
   In a large bowl, whisk together flour, baking soda, baking powder, cinnamon, nutmeg, ginger, and salt.
3. **Wet Ingredients:**
   In another bowl, whisk pumpkin puree, applesauce, maple syrup, egg whites, vanilla, and almond milk until smooth.
4. **Combine and Bake:**
   Gradually add wet ingredients to dry, stirring just until combined. Pour batter into prepared pan, smooth the top, and bake for 45-50 minutes, until a toothpick comes out clean. Let cool in pan for 10 minutes, then transfer to a wire rack.
5. **Make and Apply Glaze:**
   Whisk maple syrup, powdered sugar (or monk fruit powder), and almond milk until smooth. Drizzle glaze over cooled loaf, garnishing with pecans and cinnamon if desired.

Nutr. (Per Serving): Calories: 180 | Prot: 4g | Carbs: 30g | Fat: 4g | Fiber: 4g | Chol: 0mg | Na: 200mg | K: 240mg

Pear Tart with Vanilla Filling (Almond Flour)

Ingredients:

For the Almond Crust:
- 1 1/4 cups almond flour
- 2 tbsp coconut oil, melted
- 1 tbsp pure maple syrup
- 1/4 tsp salt

For the Vanilla Filling:
- 1/2 cup unsweetened almond milk
- 2 tbsp cornstarch
- 2 tbsp maple syrup
- 1 tsp vanilla extract

For the Topping:
- 2 ripe pears, thinly sliced
- 1 tbsp lemon juice
- 1 tbsp maple syrup (for brushing)

Garnishes (optional):
- A sprinkle of powdered sugar
- Fresh mint leaves

Instructions:

1. **Preheat Oven:**
   Preheat oven to 350°F (175°C). Lightly grease a small tart pan or line with parchment paper.
2. **Prepare Almond Crust:**
   Mix almond flour, coconut oil, maple syrup, and salt until it forms a crumbly dough. Press evenly into tart pan and bake for 10-12 minutes until golden. Let cool.
3. **Make Vanilla Filling:**
   In a saucepan, whisk almond milk, cornstarch, maple syrup, and vanilla. Cook over medium heat, stirring until thickened (5-7 minutes). Let cool slightly.
4. **Assemble Tart:**
   Pour filling into cooled crust and spread evenly. Arrange pear slices decoratively on top, overlapping slightly. Brush with lemon juice and drizzle with maple syrup.
5. **Bake:**
   Bake tart for 15 minutes until pears are tender. Let cool before serving.
6. **Garnish and Serve:**
   Dust with powdered sugar and garnish with mint if desired. Slice and enjoy!

Nutr. (Per Serving): Calories: 220 | Prot: 5g | Carbs: 24g | Fat: 13g | Fiber: 4g | Chol: 0mg | Na: 90mg | K: 210mg

Cookies with Dates, Oats, and Almonds

⏱ 10 min   🍳 15 min   🔔 4 svgs.

Ingredients:

- 1 cup old-fashioned rolled oats
- 1/2 cup almond flour
- 1/2 cup pitted dates, finely chopped
- 1/4 cup slivered almonds
- 1/4 cup unsweetened applesauce
- 2 tbsp maple syrup or honey
- 1 tsp vanilla extract
- 1/2 tsp ground cinnamon
- 1/4 tsp baking soda
- Pinch of salt

Customizable Ingredients:
- Add 1 tbsp flaxseeds or chia seeds for extra fiber
- Replace dates with dried apricots or raisins for a variation in flavor

Instructions:

1.Preheat the Oven:

Preheat your oven to 350°F (175°C). Line a baking sheet with parchment paper or lightly grease it with nonstick spray.

2.Mix the Dry Ingredients:

In a large bowl, combine the rolled oats, almond flour, cinnamon, baking soda, and salt. Stir to evenly distribute the dry ingredients.

3.Prepare the Wet Ingredients:

In a separate bowl, whisk together the applesauce, maple syrup (or honey), and vanilla extract until smooth.

4.Combine the Mixtures:

Pour the wet ingredients into the dry ingredients. Stir until well combined. Fold in the chopped dates and slivered almonds, ensuring they are evenly distributed throughout the dough.

5.Form the Cookies:

Scoop out tablespoon-sized portions of the dough and place them on the prepared baking sheet, leaving about 2 inches of space between each cookie. Flatten the dough slightly with the back of a spoon.

6.Bake:

Bake in the preheated oven for 12-15 minutes, or until the cookies are lightly golden around the edges. Remove from the oven and let the cookies cool on the baking sheet for 5 minutes before transferring to a wire rack to cool completely.

Nutr. (Per Serving): Calories: 150 | Prot: 3g | Carbs: 22g | Fat: 6g | Fiber: 4g | Chol: 0mg | Na: 60mg | K: 180mg

Mango and Passionfruit Chia Pudding

⏱ 10 min   🍳 0 min   🔔 4 svgs.

Ingredients:

- 1/4 cup chia seeds
- 1 cup unsweetened almond milk (or any plant-based milk)
- 1 tbsp pure maple syrup (optional, for sweetness)
- 1 tsp vanilla extract
- 1 large ripe mango, peeled and diced
- 2 passionfruits (pulp scooped out)
- Fresh mint leaves (optional, for garnish)

Customizable Ingredients:
- Add 1 tbsp shredded coconut for added texture
- Substitute mango with pineapple or papaya for a different tropical twist

Instructions:

1.Prepare the Chia Pudding Base:

In a mixing bowl, whisk together the chia seeds, almond milk, maple syrup (if using), and vanilla extract. Make sure the chia seeds are well distributed to avoid clumping.

2.Chill the Pudding:

Cover the bowl and place it in the refrigerator for at least 4 hours, or overnight, to allow the chia seeds to absorb the liquid and thicken into a pudding-like consistency.

3.Prepare the Mango Puree:

While the chia pudding is chilling, blend the diced mango in a blender or food processor until smooth. Set aside.

4.Assemble the Pudding:

Once the chia pudding has set, stir it gently to ensure even consistency. Divide the chia pudding evenly into serving glasses or bowls. Layer the mango puree on top of the chia pudding.

5.Top with Passionfruit:

Scoop the fresh passionfruit pulp over the mango puree, allowing the flavors to mingle. Garnish with fresh mint leaves for a pop of color and added freshness.

Nutr. (Per Serving): Calories: 150 | Prot: 3g | Carbs: 27g | Fat: 5g | Fiber: 7g | Chol: 0mg | Na: 40mg | K: 290mg

Oat and Banana Muffins with Cinnamon Swirl

🕐 10 min 🍳 20 min 🔔 4 svgs.

Ingredients:

For the Muffins:
- 1 cup rolled oats
- 1/2 cup whole wheat flour
- 1 tsp baking powder
- 1/2 tsp baking soda
- 1/4 tsp salt
- 2 ripe bananas, mashed
- 1/4 cup unsweetened applesauce
- 2 tbsp maple syrup or honey
- 1 tsp vanilla extract
- 1/2 cup unsweetened almond milk

For the Cinnamon Swirl:
- 1 tbsp cinnamon
- 2 tbsp maple syrup or honey

Customizable Ingredients:
- Add 1/4 cup chopped walnuts or almonds for extra crunch
- Sprinkle in 1 tbsp flaxseeds or chia seeds for additional fiber

Instructions:

1. Preheat the Oven:
 Preheat oven to 350°F (175°C). Line a muffin tin or grease with nonstick spray.
2. Prepare Dry Ingredients:
 In a large bowl, mix rolled oats, whole wheat flour, baking powder, baking soda, and salt.
3. Prepare Wet Ingredients:
 In a separate bowl, mash bananas and mix in applesauce, maple syrup (or honey), vanilla, and almond milk until smooth.
4. Combine Mixtures:
 Pour wet ingredients into dry and mix until just combined to avoid dense muffins.

5. Create Cinnamon Swirl:
 In a small bowl, mix cinnamon with maple syrup (or honey) to form a paste.
6. Fill Muffin Tin:
 Fill each muffin cup halfway with batter. Add a spoonful of cinnamon swirl, then cover with more batter. Swirl with a toothpick.
7. Bake:
 Bake for 18-20 minutes, or until a toothpick comes out clean. Let muffins cool in the tin for 5 minutes before transferring to a wire rack.

Nutr. (Per Serving): Calories: 140 | Prot: 3g | Carbs: 28g | Fat: 2g | Fiber: 4g | Chol: 0mg | Na: 130mg | K: 250mg

---

Vegan Peanut Butter Cups with Dark Chocolate

🕐 10 min 🍳 20 min 🔔 4 svgs.

Ingredients:

For the Chocolate Layer:
- 1/2 cup dark chocolate (70% cacao or higher), melted
- 1 tsp coconut oil

For the Peanut Butter Filling:
- 1/4 cup natural peanut butter (no added sugar or salt)
- 1 tbsp maple syrup or agave syrup
- 1/4 tsp vanilla extract

Garnishes (optional):
- A pinch of sea salt for sprinkling on top
- Chopped peanuts for texture

Customizable Ingredients:
- Swap peanut butter for almond or sunflower seed butter for a different flavor.
- Add a touch of cinnamon or cocoa powder to the filling for extra richness.

Instructions:

1. Prepare the Chocolate Layer:
 Melt the dark chocolate and coconut oil together in a heatproof bowl over a pot of simmering water (double boiler method), or use a microwave in 20-second intervals, stirring in between until smooth.
2. Fill the Muffin Liners:
 Line a muffin tin with small paper liners. Spoon about 1 teaspoon of the melted chocolate mixture into each liner, spreading it evenly over the bottom. Place the tin in the freezer for 5 minutes to allow the chocolate to harden.
3. Make the Peanut Butter Filling:
 In a small bowl, combine the peanut butter, maple syrup (or

agave), and vanilla extract. Stir until smooth and creamy.
4. Assemble the Peanut Butter Cups:
 Remove muffin tin from freezer. Add 1 tsp peanut butter filling to each chocolate layer, flattening slightly without touching edges.
5. Spoon remaining chocolate over filling to cover.
 Once all the cups are assembled, return the muffin tin to the freezer for 10-15 minutes until the chocolate has fully set.
6. Garnish and Serve:
 Remove the peanut butter cups from the freezer, sprinkle a pinch of sea salt or chopped peanuts on top if desired, and enjoy!

Nutr. (Per Serving): Calories: 150 | Prot: 4g | Carbs: 10g | Fat: 10g | Fiber: 3g | Chol: 0mg | Na: 50mg | K: 150mg

Chilled Pineapple Coconut Panna Cotta (Dairy-Free)

⏱ 10 min 🍳 180 min 🛎 4 svgs.

Ingredients:

For the Coconut Panna Cotta:
- 1 1/4 cups light coconut milk (unsweetened)
- 1/4 cup almond milk
- 2 tbsp pure maple syrup or agave syrup
- 1 tsp vanilla extract
- 1 1/2 tsp agar-agar powder (or 1 tsp gelatin for non-vegan option)

For the Pineapple Topping:
- 1 cup fresh pineapple, finely diced
- 2 tbsp pure maple syrup or agave syrup
- 1 tbsp lime juice

Garnishes (optional):
- Fresh mint leaves
- Toasted coconut flakes

Instructions:

1. Prepare the Coconut Panna Cotta:
 In a small saucepan, combine the coconut milk, almond milk, maple syrup, and vanilla extract. Stir in the agar-agar powder and whisk well to dissolve. Bring the mixture to a gentle boil over medium heat, whisking continuously. Once it reaches a boil, reduce the heat and simmer for 2-3 minutes, allowing the agar-
2. agar to fully activate.

Set the Panna Cotta:
 Remove the mixture from heat and pour it into small glass jars or ramekins. Let them cool to room temperature, then transfer to the refrigerator to chill for at least 3 hours, or until set.

3. Prepare the Pineapple Topping:
 In a blender, combine the diced pineapple, maple syrup, and lime juice. Blend until smooth to create a fresh pineapple sauce. If you prefer a chunkier texture, you can pulse it a few times to leave small pieces.

4. Assemble the Panna Cotta:
 Once the coconut panna cotta has fully set, spoon the pineapple topping evenly over each jar or ramekin. Garnish with fresh mint leaves and a sprinkle of toasted coconut flakes if desired.

Nutr. (Per Serving): Calories: 150 | Prot: 1g | Carbs: 22g | Fat: 6g | Fiber: 2g | Chol: 0mg | Na: 15mg | K: 160mg

Vanilla Almond Milk Pudding with Fresh Raspberries

⏱ 10 min 🍳 120 min 🛎 4 svgs.

Ingredients:

- 2 cups unsweetened almond milk
- 3 tbsp cornstarch
- 2 tbsp pure maple syrup (or agave syrup)
- 1 tsp vanilla extract
- 1/4 tsp salt
- 1/2 cup fresh raspberries

Garnishes (optional):
- Sliced almonds
- Fresh mint leaves

Instructions:

1. Prepare the Pudding Base:
 In a small bowl, whisk together the cornstarch and 1/4 cup of almond milk until smooth to create a slurry.
2. Heat the Almond Milk:
 In a medium saucepan, heat the remaining almond milk, maple syrup, vanilla extract, and salt over medium heat. Stir frequently to avoid scorching.
3. Thicken the Pudding:
 Once the almond milk mixture is warm, whisk in the cornstarch slurry. Continue cooking, stirring constantly, until the mixture thickens and begins to bubble, about 5-7 minutes.

4. Chill the Pudding:
 Remove the saucepan from heat and let the pudding cool slightly. Pour the pudding into serving jars or bowls. Cover and refrigerate for at least 2 hours, or until fully chilled and set.
5. Serve with Fresh Raspberries:
 Once the pudding is chilled, top each serving with fresh raspberries. Garnish with sliced almonds or fresh mint leaves for added texture and flavor.

Nutr. (Per Serving): Calories: 120 | Prot: 1g | Carbs: 18g | Fat: 3g | Fiber: 3g | Chol: 0mg | Na: 100mg | K: 160mg

Peach and Coconut Cream Parfait

Ingredients:

- 1 can (14 oz) full-fat coconut milk (refrigerated overnight)
- 2 tbsp pure maple syrup or honey
- 1 tsp vanilla extract
- 3 ripe peaches, sliced
- 1/4 cup toasted coconut flakes (for garnish)
- Fresh mint leaves (optional, for garnish)

Customizable Ingredients:
- Add 1/4 cup granola or crushed nuts for added texture.
- Swap peaches for nectarines or mango for a different flavor twist.

Instructions:

1.Prepare the Coconut Cream:
  Open the can of chilled coconut milk and scoop out the solid cream from the top into a mixing bowl (leaving the liquid behind). Add the maple syrup (or honey) and vanilla extract. Using a hand mixer or whisk, whip the coconut cream until light and fluffy, about 2-3 minutes.

2.Layer the Parfait:
  In serving glasses, add a layer of the whipped coconut cream at the bottom, followed by a layer of sliced peaches. Repeat the layering process until the glasses are filled, ending with a layer of coconut cream on top.

3.Chill the Parfaits:
  Place the parfaits in the refrigerator for about 30 minutes to allow the flavors to meld and the coconut cream to firm up.

4.Garnish and Serve:
  Before serving, sprinkle toasted coconut flakes on top and garnish with fresh mint leaves if desired.

Nutr. (Per Serving): Calories: 200 | Prot: 2g | Carbs: 20g | Fat: 13g | Fiber: 3g | Chol: 0mg | Na: 10mg | K: 300mg

Banana Bread with Walnuts

Ingredients:

- 1 1/2 cups whole wheat flour
- 1 tsp baking soda
- 1/4 tsp salt
- 3 ripe bananas, mashed
- 1/4 cup unsweetened applesauce
- 1/4 cup pure maple syrup or honey
- 1 tsp vanilla extract
- 1/2 cup chopped walnuts (plus extra for topping)
- 1/2 tsp ground cinnamon (optional)

Customizable Ingredients:
- Add 1/4 cup raisins or dark chocolate chips for extra flavor.
- Swap walnuts for pecans or almonds for a different nutty twist.

Instructions:

1.Preheat the Oven:
  Preheat your oven to 350°F (175°C). Grease a 9x5-inch loaf pan or line it with parchment paper for easy removal.

2.Mix the Dry Ingredients:
  In a large bowl, whisk together the whole wheat flour, baking soda, salt, and ground cinnamon (if using).

3.Prepare the Wet Ingredients:
  In another bowl, mash the ripe bananas and stir in the applesauce, maple syrup (or honey), and vanilla extract until smooth.

4.Combine the Mixtures:
  Gradually add the wet ingredients to the dry ingredients, stirring gently until just combined. Be careful not to overmix. Fold in the chopped walnuts.

5.Bake the Banana Bread:
  Pour the batter into the prepared loaf pan and smooth the top. Sprinkle extra walnuts on top for added crunch. Bake for 50-55 minutes, or until a toothpick inserted into the center comes out clean.

6.Cool and Serve:
  Allow the banana bread to cool in the pan for 10 minutes before transferring it to a wire rack to cool completely. Slice and enjoy!

Nutr. (Per Serving): Calories: 220 | Prot: 5g | Carbs: 35g | Fat: 7g | Fiber: 4g | Chol: 0mg | Na: 200mg | K: 300mg

Lemon Chia Poppy Seed Muffins

⏱ 10 min   🍳 20 min   🍽 4 svgs.

Ingredients:

- 1 cup whole wheat flour
- 1/4 cup chia seeds
- 1 tbsp poppy seeds
- 1 tsp baking powder
- 1/2 tsp baking soda
- 1/4 tsp salt
- 1/4 cup unsweetened applesauce
- 1/4 cup pure maple syrup or honey
- 1/2 cup unsweetened almond milk
- 2 tbsp fresh lemon juice
- 1 tbsp lemon zest (from 1 lemon)
- 1 tsp vanilla extract

Customizable Ingredients:
- Add 1/4 cup chopped nuts like almonds or walnuts for extra crunch.
- For more lemon flavor, add 1/2 tsp lemon extract.

Instructions:

1.Preheat the Oven:
 Preheat your oven to 350°F (175°C) and line a muffin tin with paper liners or lightly grease with nonstick spray.
2.Mix the Dry Ingredients:
 In a large bowl, combine the whole wheat flour, chia seeds, poppy seeds, baking powder, baking soda, and salt. Stir well to ensure all the dry ingredients are evenly distributed.
3.Prepare the Wet Ingredients:
 In a separate bowl, whisk together the applesauce, maple syrup (or honey), almond milk, fresh lemon juice, lemon zest, and vanilla extract.
4.Combine the Mixtures:

Pour the wet ingredients into the dry ingredients and stir until just combined. Be careful not to overmix, as this can affect the texture of the muffins.
5.Fill the Muffin Tin:
 Evenly divide the batter among the muffin cups, filling each about three-quarters full.
6.Bake the Muffins and Serve::
 Place the muffin tin in the preheated oven and bake for 18-20 minutes, or until a toothpick inserted into the center of a muffin comes out clean.Remove the muffins from the oven and let them cool in the tin for 5 minutes before transferring to a wire rack to cool completely.

Nutr. (Per Serving): Calories: 140 | Prot: 3g | Carbs: 25g | Fat: 4g | Fiber: 4g | Chol: 0mg | Na: 150mg | K: 100mg

Carrot Cake with Cashew Cream Frosting

⏱ 15 min   🍳 30 min   🍽 4 svgs.

Ingredients:

For the Carrot Cake:
- 1 cup whole wheat flour
- 1/2 tsp baking powder
- 1/2 tsp baking soda
- 1/2 tsp ground cinnamon
- 1/4 tsp ground ginger
- 1/4 tsp salt
- 1/4 cup unsweetened applesauce
- 1/4 cup pure maple syrup
- 1 tsp vanilla extract
- 2 large carrots, grated
- 1/4 cup chopped walnuts (optional)

For the Cashew Cream Frosting:
- 1/2 cup raw cashews (soaked for 4 hours or overnight)
- 2 tbsp pure maple syrup
- 1/2 tsp vanilla extract
- 1 tbsp lemon juice
- 1/4 cup unsweetened almond milk

Garnishes (optional):
- Extra chopped walnuts
- A sprinkle of ground cinnamon

Instructions:

1.Preheat the Oven:
 Preheat your oven to 350°F (175°C). Grease a small 8-inch cake pan or line it with parchment paper.
2.Mix the Dry Ingredients:
 In a medium bowl, whisk together the whole wheat flour, baking powder, baking soda, cinnamon, ginger, and salt.
3.Combine the Wet Ingredients:
 In a separate bowl, mix applesauce, maple syrup, and vanilla until smooth. Stir in grated carrots and walnuts (if using).
4.Combine the Mixtures:
 Gradually add dry ingredients to wet mixture, stirring gently until just combined.

5.Bake the Cake:
 Pour batter into prepared pan and bake for 25-30 minutes, until a toothpick comes out clean. Let cool completely.
Prepare the Cashew Cream Frosting:
6.Drain the soaked cashews and add them to a blender along with the maple syrup, vanilla extract, lemon juice, and almond milk. Blend until smooth and creamy, adding more almond milk as needed to reach the desired consistency.
7.Frost the Cake:
 Spread frosting over cooled cake. Garnish with chopped walnuts and a sprinkle of cinnamon if desired.

Nutr. (Per Serving): Calories: 230 | Prot: 6g | Carbs: 32g | Fat: 8g | Fiber: 5g | Chol: 0mg | Na: 150mg | K: 250mg

Avocado Chocolate Mousse with Fresh Berries

Ingredients:

- 2 ripe avocados
- 1/4 cup unsweetened cocoa powder
- 1/4 cup pure maple syrup or honey
- 1 tsp vanilla extract
- 1/4 cup almond milk (or other plant-based milk)
- A pinch of sea salt
- 1/2 cup fresh mixed berries (strawberries, raspberries, blueberries)

Customizable Ingredients:
- Add 1/2 tsp ground cinnamon or espresso powder for extra depth of flavor.
- Swap maple syrup for agave or another natural sweetener.

Instructions:

1.Prepare the Mousse:
  Scoop the flesh of the ripe avocados into a blender or food processor. Add the unsweetened cocoa powder, maple syrup (or honey), vanilla extract, almond milk, and a pinch of sea salt. Blend until smooth and creamy, scraping down the sides as needed.

2.Adjust Consistency:
  If the mousse is too thick, add a little more almond milk, one tablespoon at a time, until you reach your desired consistency.

3.Chill the Mousse:
  Transfer the mousse to serving bowls or glasses. Place in the refrigerator for at least 15 minutes to chill and allow the flavors to meld.

4.Top with Fresh Berries:
  Once chilled, top each serving with a mix of fresh berries. You can also add a sprinkle of shredded coconut or chopped nuts for extra texture if desired.

Nutr. (Per Serving): Calories: 220 | Prot: 3g | Carbs: 25g | Fat: 13g | Fiber: 8g | Chol: 0mg | Na: 30mg | K: 550mg

Rhubarb and Strawberry Pie

Ingredients:

For the Crust:
- 1 1/2 cups whole wheat flour
- 1/4 cup cold coconut oil (or vegan butter)
- 1/4 cup cold water
- 1 tbsp pure maple syrup (or honey)
- A pinch of salt

For the Filling:
- 2 cups fresh rhubarb, chopped
- 2 cups fresh strawberries, sliced
- 1/4 cup pure maple syrup or honey
- 2 tbsp cornstarch (or arrowroot powder)
- 1 tbsp fresh lemon juice
- 1 tsp vanilla extract
- 1/2 tsp ground cinnamon (optional)

Garnishes (optional):
- Fresh mint leaves
- A sprinkle of powdered sugar or coconut flakes

Instructions:

1.Prepare the Crust:
  In a bowl, mix flour and salt. Add cold coconut oil or vegan butter, blending until crumbly. Add maple syrup (or honey) and cold water until dough forms. Shape into a ball, wrap in plastic, and refrigerate for 15 minutes.

2.Make Filling & Preheat Oven:
  Preheat oven to 375°F (190°C). In a large bowl, combine rhubarb, strawberries, maple syrup (or honey), cornstarch, lemon juice, vanilla, and cinnamon (if using). Toss until coated. Grease or line a 9-inch pie dish.

3.Roll Out Dough & Assemble Pie:
  Roll out chilled dough on a floured surface and transfer to the pie dish, pressing gently. Pour the filling into the crust. Use any leftover dough to create a lattice or leave open.

4.Bake Pie:
  Bake for 40-45 minutes until filling is bubbly and crust is golden. Cover edges with foil if they brown too quickly.

5.Cool & Serve:
  Let cool for 30 minutes before slicing. Serve warm or at room temperature, garnished with powdered sugar or mint.

Nutr. (Per Serving): Calories: 230 | Prot: 4g | Carbs: 35g | Fat: 9g | Fiber: 6g | Chol: 0mg | Na: 110mg | K: 300mg

Scan the QR Code Below to Claim Your Free Bonus!

To thank you for purchasing the Low Cholesterol Diet Cookbook for Beginners, we're excited to offer you **a 4-week meal plan and motivational guide designed to support** your journey to better health.

How to Access Your Bonus:

1. **Scan** the QR code below using your smartphone or tablet.
2. **Enter your email address** in the form provided.
3. **Open the link** that appears after you submit the form and download your bonus materials.

Enjoy your journey to a healthier, low-cholesterol lifestyle!

If you experience any issues scanning the QR code or accessing your bonus materials, please contact the author at the email provided below:

Yolanda.gill.author@gmail.com

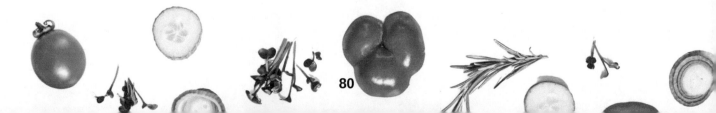

CONCLUSION

Embarking on a low-cholesterol diet is not just about what you eat—it's about creating a balanced and fulfilling lifestyle that supports your overall well-being. The journey to better heart health is a long one, but it doesn't have to be restrictive or boring. Maintaining a balance between health and flavor is key, and with the tools and recipes in this cookbook, you have everything you need to create meals that are as delicious as they are nutritious.

Remember, the goal is not perfection but progress. Progress can look like small, tangible changes—such as incorporating more vegetables into your daily meals, reducing your intake of processed foods, or successfully substituting saturated fats with healthier options. It can also mean noticing improvements in your energy levels, managing your weight more effectively, or receiving positive feedback from your healthcare provider about your cholesterol levels. Celebrate these wins, no matter how minor they may seem, as they are all steps toward a healthier heart. Continue to experiment with new flavors, enjoy your favorite meals in moderation, and keep learning about how your food choices impact your health. You have the power to make changes that will benefit not only your heart but also your energy, mood, and quality of life. Embrace this journey with confidence, creativity, and a commitment to your health. You deserve to feel your best, and every small step you take brings you closer to a healthier, happier you.

Your journey to better health is an ongoing process, filled with learning, adapting, and growing. Don't be discouraged by setbacks—every effort counts, and each positive change, no matter how small, contributes to your overall well-being. By maintaining a positive attitude, staying open to new ideas, and continually striving to make healthier choices, you will find that this lifestyle becomes second nature. The recipes, tips, and strategies shared in this cookbook are here to support you, inspire you, and remind you that taking care of your heart can be both rewarding and delicious.

Thank you for taking this journey with us. Here's to your health, your heart, and the countless delicious meals yet to come!

Made in the USA
Columbia, SC
11 April 2025

56484775R10046